Natural disasters
Acts of God
or acts of Man?

Books are to be returned on or before
the last date below.

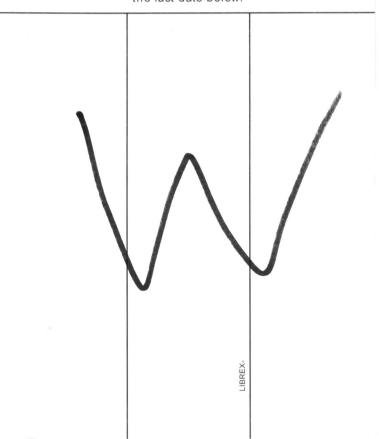

LIBREX-

© Earthscan 1984
First published 1984
Reprinted 1985
ISBN No 0-905347-54-4

Published by the International Institute for
Environment and Development, London and
Washington, DC

Typeset by Wetherby Typesetters, Wetherby, UK
Printed by Russell Press, Nottingham, UK

Cover photo: Oxfam

Earthscan receives financial support from the UN
Environment Programme, the European
Community, the Nordic aid agencies (DANIDA,
FINNIDA, NORAD and SIDA), the Netherlands
Foreign Ministry, the World Bank and the UN
Food and Agriculture Organization.

Written by Anders Wijkman, secretary general of
the Swedish Red Cross, and Lloyd Timberlake,
editorial director of Earthscan, this book follows
from a major collaborative study by both
organisations into the links between environment
and disasters, funded by the Swedish International
Development Authority. Earthscan is a news and
information service on global development and
environment issues, operated on an editorially-
independent basis by the International Institute for
Environment and Development.

 Contents

 **Acknowledgments**

This book is the result of a complex but pleasant and symbiotic collaboration between the Swedish Red Cross and Earthscan, the London-based news and information service on international environment and development issues, and all of the many individuals and groups which have aided these two organisations.

In 1982, the Swedish Red Cross began work on a study of human and environmental disasters in the Third World. Its report, *Prevention Better than Cure,* drafted by Gunnar Hagman with additional material from Henrik Beer, Martin Bendz and Anders Wijkman, was published in May 1984 and presented to an international symposium of experts and decisionmakers in the fields of disaster relief and environment in Stockholm in June.

In late 1983, Earthscan editorial director Lloyd Timberlake, with extra material and advice from British geographer Phil O'Keefe, began work on a press briefing document explaining how humans make themselves more vulnerable and their land more prone to natural disasters. That document, which drew heavily on the work of Hagman and his collaborators and which was funded by the Swedish Red Cross, was published in June 1984 at a press seminar held in conjunction with the Stockholm symposium.

Hagman's statistics showing the alarming increase in so-called "natural disasters", which formed the basis of both reports, came from the League of Red Cross and Red Crescent Societies, the US Office of Foreign Disaster Assistance (OFDA) and the United Nations Disaster Relief Co-ordinator. Other UN organisations especially helpful with documentation and advice include the UN Environment Programme, UNICEF, the World Bank, the UN Food and Agriculture Organization and the World Food Programme. The Swedish International Development Authority (SIDA), which also helps to fund Earthscan activities, provided funding and advice for the Swedish Red Cross report.

This book is based on both the Earthscan and the Swedish Red Cross reports and contains extra material which became available at the Stockholm symposium. It was edited and produced by Jon Tinker, Barbara Cheney, Clare McCormack and Rebecca Fowler of Earthscan, and financially supported by the Swedish Red Cross with funds from SIDA.

 **Summary**

Introduction: A question of balance

The common view of 'natural disasters' is due for a radical change. Though triggered by natural events such as floods and earthquakes, disasters are increasingly man-made. Some disasters (flood, drought, famine) are caused more by environmental and resource mismanagement than by too much or too little rainfall. The impact of other disasters, which are triggered by acts of nature (earthquake, volcano, hurricane) are magnified by unwise human actions. Disasters are social and political events which can be and often are prevented. In the Third World where the poor are forced to overuse their land and live on dangerous ground, disasters are taking a rising toll. By emphasising mitigation instead of development, current disaster relief is often inadequate to the task it sets itself.

Chapter 1: Forces of nature, acts of Man

The ratio for major disasters per year are: 15 (Asia); 10 (Latin America and Africa); and 1 (Europe and Australia). Floods and droughts are the most important cause of disasters in terms of human impact, followed by hurricanes, earthquakes, volcanoes and tsunami. Disasters have increased sharply in number and death toll over the last two decades. Yet there is no evidence that natural 'disaster triggers' are becoming either more frequent or more dangerous. Poor people in poor countries are most vulnerable to disasters. There are over 3,000 deaths per disaster in low-income countries, compared with 500 in high-income countries. The three major contributors to disasters in the Third World are poverty and inequality, environmental degradation and rapid population growth.

Chapter 2: Droughts: too little water

Lack of rain is not the sole cause of drought. Deforested and overused tropical soils erode easily, retaining insufficient water. Reduced rainfall may trigger a drought, but human pressure on the land is the primary cause. In many Third World countries, economic policies which discriminate against the rural poor are intensifying this pressure. By contrast, government support and subsidies for US farmers spread the burden of drought over taxpayers and consumers. Drought is not the sole cause of famine. Where people can respond flexibly to drought, disaster is minimised. Third World governments have often impaired this flexibility, discouraging migration, replacing diversified subsistence agriculture with a single cash crop. Foreign aid often fails to reach those hardest hit by drought.

Chapter 3: Floods

Floods are increasing more rapidly than any other type of disaster. Tropical deforestation and erosion contribute to the flood hazard in the Himalayas, the Andes and in China. The poor are exposed to the greatest danger. They are relegated to the most flood-prone land, and are afforded little of the flood-control protection which the rich may enjoy. Relief and rehabilitation programmes may actually encourage poor people to remain in flood-endangered areas.

Chapter 4: Tropical cyclones and other winds

Tropical windstorms are 'acts of God', so far uninfluenced by human intervention. But the destructive effects of the storm surges which they cause have been increased by deforestation. Due to inadequate communication systems, the poor do not benefit from early warnings and suffer disproportionate death and damage. Many Third World cities contain large shantytowns near the shore or crowded against rivers prone to flooding.

Chapter 5: Earthquakes

Earthquakes are the most poorly understood and predicted of all the natural disasters. Much Third World urban housing is vulnerable to earthquakes, often badly-constructed and sited on unstable steep slopes. Frequently built on illegally occupied land, it is not subject to planning regulations. In the North, strictly-enforced building codes and zoning laws make earthquake-prone cities less and less vulnerable. Such measures depend on a level of affluence which does not extend to the South's poor.

Chapter 6: Tsunami and volcanoes

Environmental destruction of sea-front dunes, coral reefs and mangrove forests has increased the vulnerability of Pacific coastal villages to tsunami (tidal waves). Land in the vicinity of volcanoes is often densely populated, because the volcanoes are on islands, or because people intensively cultivate the rich volcanic soil.

Chapter 7: Relief

Disaster aid from Northern governments sometimes tends to conform to the donor country's foreign policy rather than to the recipient country's need. Much 'relief' is merely the export of surplus food and materials which are inappropriate for the disaster conditions. When the surplus in the donor country dries up, so does the aid. Biases in disaster relief dictate that sudden, dramatic, 'newsworthy' catastrophes tend to receive more aid than disasters which grind people down slowly. Food aid saves lives but can also undermine long-term local self-sufficiency. When injudiciously supplied it can disrupt local markets and make food too expensive for the poor. Free food may act as an incentive to corruption and in the long term may actually increase starvation. Some critics of relief operations claim that their main goal is to return victims to the status quo. Yet it is the status quo which makes them disaster-prone and vulnerable.

Chapter 8: Disasters and development

Effective disaster mitigation and prevention depends on long-term planning for development toward a more sustainable and less vulnerable society. Some relief agencies are embarking on new types of community-based disaster prevention programmes. Improved self-reliance in respect of food and fuel, access to land, employment, better health and nutrition, family planning and education are important components of disaster prevention. Disaster prevention and the elimination of poverty are closely linked, as are poverty and environmental degradation. Many relief agencies are beginning to complement their emergency aid with development programmes. In African drought areas they have set up seed banks, offering a choice of seed varieties that will help poor farmers cope with climatic variation. They have assisted marginal farmers to develop re-wooded catchment areas in desert lands. Simple early warning systems which monitor village markets have been set up to predict food shortages. Village flood co-operatives in Dominica have protected farmers against crop losses by cyclone insurance. It is likely that relief agencies will increasingly wish to look upon disasters as problems of development as well as problems of relief. Many of these agencies are now working to gain the knowledge, experience, trained personnel and public backing to begin to put these new ideas into practice.

Preface

by
Prince Sadruddin Aga Khan

This book, based on the perceptive report by the Swedish Red Cross entitled *Prevention Better than Cure* and on press briefing material prepared by Earthscan, adds new emphasis to the known but largely ignored principle of tackling basic causes, rather than the symptoms of catastrophes.

The price to pay for the demands imposed by mankind on our environment, extravagant to the point of profligacy, is increasing with time. It is the poorest who suffer the most, especially in the South, but all of us are caught up in the same syndrome. For we inherit but one earth. When people conspire against nature to destroy tree cover, or deplete the water table, or pollute our biosphere to the point that climatic changes occur, then the consequences, measured in terms of human suffering, are likely to be acute.

The loss of topsoil in Africa, largely as a result of the removal of tree and shrub cover, is the highest in the world. It is no wonder that per capita food production on that continent has slumped in the last decade. People are hungry; they starve, and ultimately a famine emerges. A disaster is declared, and the relief agencies swing into action. How much wiser if we could teach people to conserve their soil in the first place.

All over the planet, the great deserts of the world stretching from the Atacama on South America's western coast, to the Gobi and Takla-Makan of China and Mongolia, are expanding. Upwards of 35% of the earth's land surface is arid or semi-arid; 850 million people inhabit these areas. It is no surprise, therefore, that the Swedish Red Cross identifies drought as the disaster which affects more people on earth than any other calamity.

One can hardly doubt the validity of the main argument of this book: that we can only tackle root causes if disaster prevention and response are designed so as to incorporate both developmental and environmental strategies. Merely to bind up the wounds of suffering humanity is not enough. We must get at root causes and reverse the trends of increasing poverty and environmental degradation before it is too late. A sustainable ecosystem must be our aim, one in which the global family can live in balanced harmony with the whole of nature. The rural poor, who are the principal victims of the three elements which between them make up the major part of Third World disasters — deforestation, soil erosion and desertification — should be central to the work of all disaster agencies, whether parts of the United Nations system or non-governmental organisations. All the trends emphasise that ignorance and grinding poverty accelerate the onslaught of disasters and exacerbate the cruel impact they have, particularly on vulnerable groups of people. The poor, the handicapped, the very young and the aged are the first to lose their basic right to food, shelter and health. They need, and deserve, our help.

As the book argues, therefore, and as I certainly learned during my term in office as the UN High Commissioner for Refugees, the social development of people and their communities in disaster-prone areas has been grossly ignored by governments and agencies alike. It is not surprising that this year the United Nations has had to launch an appeal for massive amounts of food aid for 24 countries in Africa — nor that the second International Conference for Assistance to Refugees in Africa (ICARA 2) convened by the United Nations last July — highlighted the particular plight of the uprooted, the homeless and the dispossessed in the same continent.

Such appalling human conditions can best be fought through the weapons of self-reliance, literacy, preventive health care and equitable pricing structures for rural food producers — that is, helping people to respond to their own basic needs, within their environment. However bleak or alien that environment may appear to be to others, to them it remains 'home'.

These issues, in fact, are central to the work of 'The Independent Commission on International Humanitarian Issues', which Crown Prince Hassan of Jordan and I have the privilege of co-chairing. The interplay between human disaster and the environment, both social and ecological, is one of the fundamental elements in our programme on research. It is of utmost importance that more appropriate solutions and more effective responses to such disasters are sought by the international community.

I am sure that the readers will find the publication of this book and the initiative taken by the Swedish Red Cross both timely and apposite. The League of Red Cross and Red Crescent Societies are pioneers in disaster prevention and response. To embrace basic social and cultural development, as well as ecological and environmental policies, could have incalculable benefits for suffering humanity. It is an initiative which all of us would do well to support.

Prince Sadruddin Aga Khan
September 1984

(Prince Sadruddin Aga Khan is co-chairman of the Independent Commission on International Humanitarian Issues, and from 1965 until 1977 was UN High Commissioner for Refugees. He writes here in a personal capacity.)

Introduction

A question of balance

Events called "natural disasters" are killing more and more people every year. Yet there is no evidence that the climatological mechanisms associated with droughts, floods and cyclones are changing. And no geologist is claiming that the earth movements associated with earthquakes, volcanoes and tsunami (earthquake waves) are becoming more violent.

If nature is not changing, why are "natural disasters" becoming more frequent, more deadly and more destructive?

This book sets out to show that it is because people are changing their environment to make it more *prone* to some disasters, and are behaving so as to make themselves more *vulnerable* to those hazards. Growing Third World populations are forced to overcultivate, deforest and generally overuse their land, making it more prone to both floods and droughts. Growing numbers of Third World poor are forced to live on dangerous ground: in shantytowns in flood-prone river basins or foreshores, or in huts of heavy mud-brick on steep hills in earthquake-prone cities.

The common view of "natural disasters" is due for a radical change. A new term may even be needed, such as "nature disaster", to distinguish calamities associated with the forces of nature from such tribulations as war and factory explosions. Today humans are playing too large a role in natural disasters for us to go on calling them "natural".

So a distinction must be made between the "trigger events" — too little rain, too much rain, earthshocks, hurricanes —which may be natural, and the associated disasters, which may be largely man-made. For instance, a strong earthquake in an unoccupied desert area, which affects no one, is hardly a disaster. A mild earthquake in a shantytown of heavy mud-brick houses on the side of a steep ravine may well prove a disaster in terms of human deaths and suffering. But is the disaster more the result of the earthshocks or of the fact that people are living in such dangerous houses on such dangerous ground? Viewed another way, is it easier to prevent the earthshock or improve the housing conditions?

Scientists, politicians, decisionmakers and the general public have been very slow to make the basic distinction between the trigger and the disaster.

Most of the scientific effort and money devoted to natural disasters has been spent on studying climatological and geological triggers —over which humans have very little control —rather than on studying the wide range of human actions — over which humans do have some control — which bring

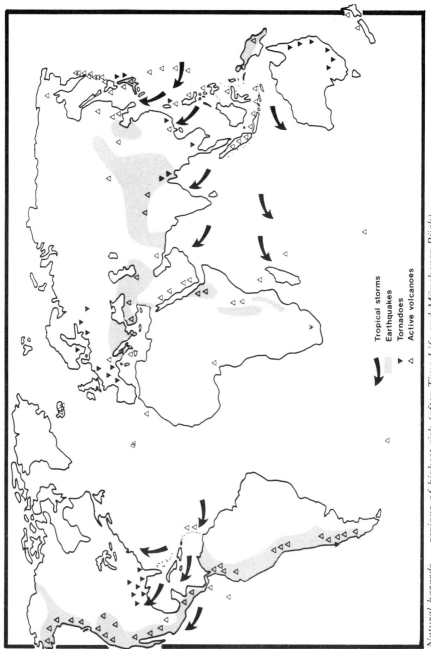

Natural hazards — regions of highest risk (after Time-Life and Münchener Rück).

Tropical storms
Earthquakes
Tornadoes
Active volcanoes

A hillside shantytown in the Dominican Republic. The rich live in sturdy houses; the houses of the poor collapse in high winds and the metal roofing sheets become lethal flying objects. As numbers of poor increase, 'hurricane disasters' increase.

more disasters upon people every year.

Contemporary natural disasters research has become "the single greatest impediment to improvement in both the understanding of natural calamities and the strategies to alleviate them", charges Canadian geographer Kenneth Hewitt.

Researchers tend to study only the physical events, and these events are technically very complex. "In practice, then, natural hazards have been carefully roped off from the rest of man-environment relations", writes Hewitt. "There is no place for any sort of 'grass roots' input; no way for any but the 'experts' to break into the technical monologue."

Yet floods and droughts are grass roots phenomena which disrupt the lives of millions of people each year, the majority of these victims relying on the "grass roots" of subsistence agriculture. Droughts affected 24.4 million people a year during the 1970s; floods affected 15.4 million. Such huge numbers, if nothing else, make such calamities a part of everyday human ecology.

Because researchers have concentrated on the physical aspects of disasters, rather than the social and political aspects, governments have been lured into putting their trust in grand physical prevention and mitigation measures:

dams, early warning systems, satellite monitoring. These have had little effect in the Third World.

But then our whole perception of the concept of a "disaster" has much more to do with social and political conditioning than with logic.

All major disasters throughout the 1970s killed over 142,000 people a year on average. Yet each year some 15 million children die of malnutrition-related causes, and nowhere is this carnage described as a disaster. The deaths of these children are predictable; governments and their agents in the fields of health and welfare know which infants are at risk. UN organisations have recently devised relatively inexpensive ways of preventing about half of these deaths. As yet there is little indication that governments and agencies will put up the necessary money. It appears that this non-stop disaster is politically and socially acceptable.

In contrast, droughts hit the US Great Plains once every 20 years or so. They remain entirely unpredictable. Yet American opinion is unanimous that deaths by starvation of US farmers are politically unacceptable. So the impact of these droughts is spread, largely by the tax system, throughout the US population. A drought there is not left to climatologists. Many government agencies are busy pushing agricultural practices, mainly soil and water conservation measures, which prevent the worst effects of drought, and providing various kinds of relief when drought does come. One hundred years ago people in the midwestern United States died of famine; today they do not.

Yet experts and organisations concerned with disasters in the Third World continue to concentrate on climate monitoring, radar tracking of cyclones and the building of barriers against flooding. These have their place. But if they consume a disproportionate amount of money and effort — if they serve as an excuse to ignore the hazards built into the victims' societies which make disasters worse — then they can do more harm than good.

Paradoxically, the organisations which have the most experience with natural disasters, the governmental and non-governmental aid and relief agencies, tend to treat them as "unnatural" events — as events somehow "off the scale" of natural daily occurrences. This attitude excuses "unnatural acts" on the part of these agencies. Thus a relief agency from one part of the planet may routinely barge into the workings of a complex society elsewhere on the planet, and interfere with the food, clothing, housing and business activities of that society without in any way being answerable to the people with whom it is interfering.

The recipients of such "relief", once the excitement has died down and they have had time to examine the results of the aid, are often very displeased. But by then no one is listening to them. In fact, they were not being listened to at the height of the relief effort. If a relief organisation makes mistakes, the victims — both of the disaster and of those mistakes — have no one to appeal to for redress.

M. Goldwater/Network

Eritrean rebels bringing food supplies into the drought-struck region from the north. More and more of Africa's 'natural disasters' are complicated by political strife.

The relief organisations themselves are beginning to realise that traditional relief operations are not enough. Red Cross agencies especially are mounting more relief efforts than ever before, yet their finances and personnel are being overwhelmed by the mounting number of disasters. Henrik Beer, who has served as secretary general both of the Swedish Red Cross and of the International League of Red Cross and Red Crescent Societies, has probably signed more disaster relief appeals than any other human being; yet he said recently that ''I have felt a growing frustration over the fact that what has been done has had, in many cases, only superficial effects, more cosmetic than profound''.

The general public's impression of disasters is formed not by relief agencies but by journalists, who are rarely experts in this area, but who are often called upon to interpret quickly both the event and the relief efforts for the rest of the world. In the aftermath of an earthquake or cyclone, there are so many tales of suffering and heroism, one rarely has time to focus on the basic causes of the damage and death.

Journalists generally hate to appear naive. If toxic foods are sold, reporters will tend to dig until they find out why such a thing happened, and which organisations and individuals allowed it. Yet journalists often innocently accept the view that high winds and water killed so many thousand victims of a given cyclone. They do not dig to see why so many people were allowed to live in such dangerous houses exposed to a storm surge, indeed why they could not live anywhere else.

Journalists may also be willing to accept the view that flying in hundreds of prefabricated houses is cost-effective charity which will relieve post-cyclone suffering. They may give such an effort a great deal of space in their articles. Yet it is always worth asking hard questions about whether a relief operation makes sense in a given society. Many, though meaning well, do not.

This book stresses a few basic thoughts about disasters and how to cope with them.

* Natural disasters are an integral part of human life, especially in the Third World. Their impact is affected by people's relations to their environment, to their government and to the other institutions of their society.
* Everyday acts by humans — farming, cutting fuelwood, building homes, choosing sites for housing — can make their land more or less prone to calamity and the people more or less vulnerable.
* Current disaster relief may not be the most charitable, efficient or most cost-effective means of alleviating the human suffering caused by disasters. It can even, in some circumstances, do more harm than good.
* As people develop economically and politically they become less vulnerable to natural disasters. Organisations concerned with disasters must be concerned with development.

If these ideas contain any great amount of truth, then most of those agencies working with natural disasters should rethink their methods of operation.

However, in stressing the ways in which humans make their land more prone to drought and flood, and thus increase their own suffering, we do not mean to imply that unpredictable Nature does not have a key role to play in triggering these disasters.

In concentrating on how the death rates from earthquakes are higher than they need be because people are allowed to live in dangerous structures in dangerous areas, we do not mean to deny that earthquakes kill people unexpectedly in the best ordered societies.

In emphasising that a cyclone disaster is an inevitable event in the life of a Third World society, we do not mean to suggest that Northern meteorologists who study low pressure areas and their movements have no role to play in helping societies cope better with cyclones. Their work has helped to save millions of lives in societies which have the transport and communications systems to take advantage of warnings.

And in explaining how many relief efforts mounted by Northern organisations for Third World disaster victims have been inadequate — and sometimes even wrong — we do not mean to ignore or denigrate the many relief operations which have saved lives and alleviated suffering. Foreign relief assistance has an important role to play. In fact, in one type of disaster with which this book does not deal, such relief may be the only way of mitigating the suffering of the victims in the short term. These are the catastrophes in which armed conflict, often in conjunction with the so-called natural disasters, produce many refugees. Such disasters are becoming more frequent, especially in Africa of late. Relieving such disasters may be particularly difficult, because of security problems, but in many cases this relief offers the only hope of keeping the victims alive until they can become more self-reliant.

Chapter 1

Forces of nature, acts of Man

"The issue is not whether societies can adapt to
further environmental degradation, but what the
price of doing so will be."
US environmentalist Erik Eckholm
Down to Earth (1982)

Despite the death, destruction and drama of major natural disasters, they
have received surprisingly little scientific attention.

The physical sciences have been hampered by the fact that many of these
events originate in places where instruments cannot peer. Earthquakes,
generally speaking, are caused by the uneven ways in which the major plates
in the Earth's crust move against one another. But there is little real
understanding of just why they happen, when they happen, and what
determines their force. This is not surprising, as the theory of plate tectonics
has gained general scientific acceptability only over the past two decades.
Tropical cyclones grow out of a complex mix of low pressure systems and
trade winds meeting near the Equator. But despite decades of expensive
monitoring in the Gulf of Mexico, meteorologists are not able to tell when
a given storm will become a hurricane, nor to explain why it does so, nor
to predict its path accurately.

Plans to interfere physically with these two phenomena — seeding cyclones
or even bombing their centres; lubricating earthquake faults with water to
release pressure or using nuclear devices for the same purpose — are thought
by even the most enthusiastic to be as dangerous as the disasters they are
meant to mitigate.

Definitions

Science has not even had much success defining what it means by the term
"disaster". Dictionaries use words such as "misfortune" or "calamity",
implying that for there to be a disaster, people must suffer. Thus a cyclone
or a quake is not a disaster unless it kills people or damages their property.

This seems obvious, but it is not. Since 1966, the UN Educational,
Scientific and Cultural Organization (UNESCO) has listed each year's

"natural disasters" — earthquakes, tsunami (large ocean waves), storm surges and volcanic eruptions. For 1969, it listed 759 — more than any other organisation. But it named only 12 of those as "destructive disasters", suggesting that there are such things as "harmless disasters".

Other experts take almost the opposite view, defining disasters only in terms of their impact upon people. For instance, in order to produce some consistency in discussing disasters, the Natural Hazard Research Group at the University of Colorado (US) came up in 1969 with the following definition of a disaster:

* more than $1 million in damage, or
* more than 100 people dead, or
* more than 100 people injured.

This definition had the effect of separating the "disaster event" — destruction, death and injuries — from the "trigger mechanisms": high winds, earth shocks, lack of rain, excess of water, lava and high waves.

But it also served to emphasise that most of the research on "disasters" by climatologists and geologists is really on the trigger mechanisms. Other definitions of "disaster" include:

* "...an event (or series of events) which seriously disrupts normal activites" (Cisin and Clark, *Man and Society in Disaster,* 1962).
* "1,000 to 1,000,000 dead or in imminent danger of death" (*Daily Telegraph,* London, 1972).
* "...occurrence of imminent threat of widespread or severe injury or loss of life or property resulting from any natural or man-made cause..." (US Office of Emergency Preparedness, 1972).
* "...an accident on a very large scale" (Walker, Studio Vista, London, 1973).

Even the apparently concise definitions based on dollars and lives can be misleading. For instance, a tornado which destroys only a few homes may do over $1 million in damages in a wealthy US suburb, and thus be a "disaster". But a widespread typhoon might destroy hundreds of Third World huts without causing $1 million in damages, and thus not be a "disaster".

Studies on how people react to disasters did not really get under way until the Cold War between the United States and the Soviet Union during the 1950s, when the threat of nuclear war raised the need for data on how individuals and communities would react during and after a catastrophe.

This work gradually took researchers beyond studies of the event itself to a consideration of how the disaster effects could be mitigated. In 1975, Robert Kates of the Natural Hazard Research Group wrote:

Sean Sprague/Earthscan

The only land most Third World city dwellers can afford is dangerous land. When this Jakarta canal/latrine floods, the houses of the poor fill with foul water. The bank and UN headquarters in the background are unaffected.

"Not only the causes of natural disasters fall within the province of science and technology, but also in some cases their prevention, as well as organisational arrangements made for forecasting them and reducing their impact when they occur."

Though this assertion was an advance over the simple measuring of shock waves and wind speeds, it suggested that the way to cope with disasters was through technology and organisation. This view had a deep effect on the thinking of the United Nations agencies dealing with disasters: the UN Development Programme (UNDP), UNESCO, the Office of the UN Disaster Relief Co-ordinator (UNDRO) and the UN Environment Programme (UNEP). To some extent, these agencies began to apply tactics which were effective in the United States to disaster planning in the Third World, where high technology and the technocrats able to organise high-tech responses tend to be in short supply.

As interest in disasters grew, more organisations — academic, relief, charitable, development, insurance and journalistic — began to keep records. Because of the problem of definitions, no one was keeping quite the same

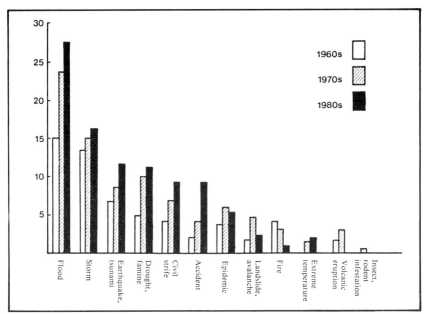

Figure 1. Average recorded annual disaster events in the world. The average number of disaster events per year (the 1980s cover only 1980-81). (Source: Prevention Better than Cure, *Swedish Red Cross, 1984, based on League of Red Cross and USOFDA statistics.)*

list. For instance, the US Office for Foreign Disaster Assistance (USOFDA) "Disaster History List" notes 1,622 events from 1900 to 1981. But the League of Red Cross and Red Crescent Societies "List of Major Appeals and Relief Actions" notes 389 events from 1919 to 1981. Both are accurate in their way. Each contains disasters the other does not list, and both have very different sets of data.

Disasters are increasing

Despite the problem of definitions, a few generalisations are possible. For instance, according to the Natural Hazard Research Group (which got much of its information directly from newspapers), Asia is the continent most prone to natural disasters; Latin America and Africa are roughly equal; and Europe and Australia are relatively unscathed. The ratios for major disasters per year are 15 (Asia); 10 (Latin America and Africa) and one (Europe and Australia).

The group ranked disasters in order of the importance of their effects on humans as follows: flood, drought, hurricane, earthquake, volcanic eruption and tsunami. (A more recent study put drought in first place. See below.)

Type of event	1960s	1970s
Drought	5.2	9.7
Flood	15.1	22.2
Civil strife/conflict	4.1	6.8
Tropical cyclone	12.1	14.5
Earthquake	6.9	8.3
Other disasters	10.8	19.5
	54.2	81.0

Figure 2. Number of recorded disaster events per year. Flood was the most frequent disaster impact during the period, and flood increased most. Tropical cyclone (included in storm events in Figure 1, of which it constitutes the major part) was the second-most common disaster agent. All major types of events appear to have increased in frequency between the 1960s and 1970s, by over 50%. (Source: Prevention Better than Cure, *Swedish Red Cross, 1984, based on League of Red Cross and USOFDA statistics.)*

The climatological disasters (flood, drought and hurricane) are also more frequent than the geological ones (earthquake, volcano and tsunami).

Drought tends to be underestimated because of difficulties in definition, monitoring, timing and the problems of distinguishing drought from the general conditions of seasonal hunger and malnutrition in much of the Third World. Earthquakes tend to be overestimated because they are easily detected at a distance. They are also more dramatic and "newsworthy" than the gradual disasters.

But the most compelling, and worrying, generalisation which can be made about natural disasters is that they are increasing, both in number and in terms of people affected.

A 1984 report by the Swedish Red Cross entitled *Prevention Better than Cure* used data from League of Red Cross and Red Crescent Societies and USOFDA lists to compare average annual disasters on a decade by decade basis. This two-year study, drafted by Gunnar Hagman, found a sharp jump in disasters from the 1960s to the 1970s, and from the 1970s to the 1980s. (The 1980s covered only 1980-81. Inclusion of the many floods and droughts of 1983 and early 1984 would have made this decade appear even more disaster-prone.)

The disasters which increased included floods, storms, earthquakes and tsunami, droughts, civil strife and accidents. Only in less important categories such as epidemic, avalanche and fire did this pattern vary (See Figures 1 and 2. The statistics on "civil strife" and "conflicts" are very dubious due to the many problems organisations face in gathering such data. However, as

Type of event	1960s	1970s
Drought	1,010	23,110
Flood	2,370	4,680
Civil strife/conflict	300	28,840
Tropical cyclone	10,750	34,360
Earthquake	5,250	38,970
Other disasters	2,890	12,960
	22,570	142,920

Figure 3. Number of people killed per year in disasters. The average annual death tolls for each type of disaster event increased over sixfold between the 1960s and 1970s. A very marked increase can be seen in all categories — greater than can be explained just by population increase. (Source: Prevention Better than Cure, *Swedish Red Cross, 1984, based on League of Red Cross and USOFDA statistics.)*

these figures play no role in this book's focus on "natural disasters", they have been accepted as provided by the USOFDA and the League.)

The average number of disasters per year was greater in the 1970s (81) than in the 1960s (54). A very great many more people died per year in disasters in the 1970s (142,820) than in the 1960s (22,570). The difference is far too great to be explained by population growth alone (see Figure 3).

Figures for the number of people affected per year also increased: 27.7 million in the 1960s and 48.3 million in the 1970s. Drought led the list, affecting 24.4 million a year in the 1970s, up from 18.5 million the previous decade. But floods showed the steepest rise, from 5.2 million in the 1960s to 15.4 million in the 1970s (Figures 4 and 5).

"Affected" is obviously an inexact word, so these figures at best indicate trends rather than offering exact numbers. But even though they do represent rough approximations, they do indicate how limited, if not misleading, are the traditional disaster definitions which measure only death tolls and property damage. The magnitude of a disaster in terms of human suffering and in terms of overall affect on the economy of a poor nation can be represented only by the inclusion of some indication of the total number of those affected. Given the number of people in poor nations living on the margin of survival, any disaster which "affects" them threatens to push them beyond that margin. (See Figure 6.)

Why are natural disasters becoming both more frequent and more dangerous to humans?

Are the "triggers" — wind, waves, rainfall, continental movements — becoming more unruly? Neither the climate (associated with drought, floods

24

Type of event	1960s	1970s
Drought	18,500,000	24,400,000
Flood	5,200,000	15,400,000
Civil strife/conflict	1,100,000	4,000,000
Tropical cyclone	2,500,000	2,800,000
Earthquake	200,000	1,200,000
Other disasters	200,000	500,000
	27,700,000	48,300,000

Figure 4 (above) and Figure 5. Number of people affected per year by disasters. Between the 1960s and 1970s, the number of people affected by disasters each year nearly doubled. (Source: Prevention Better than Cure, Swedish Red Cross, 1984, based on League of Red Cross and USOFDA statistics.)

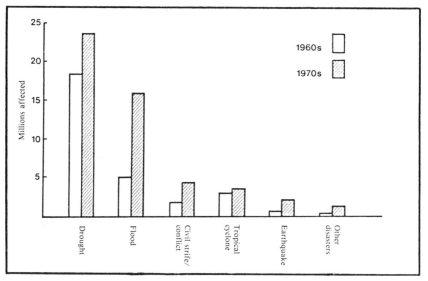

and cyclones) nor geological processes (associated with earthquakes, volcanic eruptions and tsunami) appear to be changing significantly.

Earthquakes and eruptions (both of which can cause tsunami) are easy to monitor and measure. A sensitive seismograph virtually anywhere in the world can monitor the number and magnitude of quakes anywhere on the planet. There is no evidence whatsoever that earthquakes or eruptions are becoming stronger or more frequent.

Climatic change is harder to monitor and more open to argument. Climatology is a relatively young science, and real changes in climate — as opposed to weather — need to be measured over long periods, 30 years or

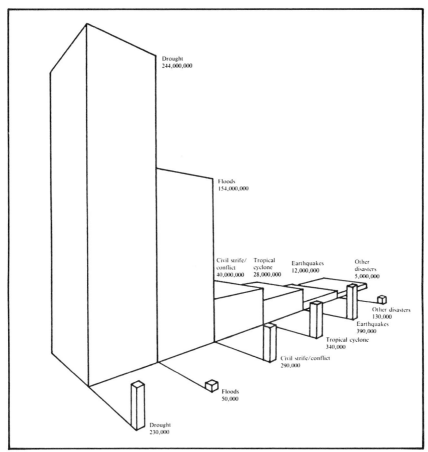

Figure 6. Disaster victims from 1970 to 1979. The large columns represent numbers affected, the smaller columns the numbers killed. (Source: Prevention Better than Cure, *Swedish Red Cross, 1984, based on USOFDA statistics.)*

so in most cases. As reliable records go back only about 120 years in the North, climatologists have little data for generalisations.

There is debate over whether the world is getting gradually colder and moving toward a new Ice Age, as a US Central Intelligence Agency report suggested, or is gradually getting warmer because of the accumulation of carbon dioxide in the atmosphere and the resultant "greenhouse effect".

Little can be said with certainty. Several recent studies have shown that rainfall in the Sahel region of Africa has never returned to levels recorded before the 1968-73 drought. US climatologist Dr F. Kenneth Hare wrote in 1983: "Several workers or groups have shown, in fact, that rainfall over inter-

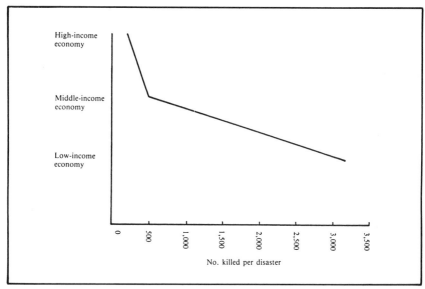

Figure 7. Disaster mortality per event (1960-81). The poorest countries have the highest mortality rate per disaster event. Middle-income countries do not have much higher death rate per disaster than the rich countries. (Source: Prevention Better than Cure, *Swedish Red Cross, 1984, based on League of Red Cross and USOFDA statistics.)*

Figure 8. Disasters seem to be most frequent in very poor and very rich areas. This is probably because disasters are often defined by property damage and loss of life: the poor countries have most loss of life, and the rich most damage to property. (Source: Interpretations of Calamity, *K. Hewitt (Ed).)*

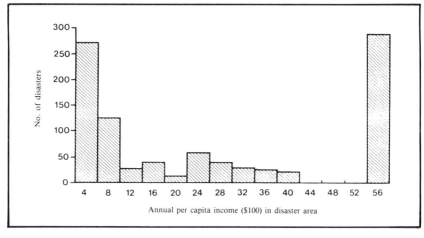

tropical Africa has declined appreciably — in some areas disastrously — in the 1960s and 1970s (the first decades of independence for many new African states)''. However, there is no scientific consensus that there have been changes in planetary climate mechanics this century likely to cause more or fiercer storms, more droughts or more floods over the long term. Thus the ''disaster triggers'' do not appear to be changing in such a way as to provide more danger for humans.

Forces of nature trigger disaster events, but can no longer be considered the main causes of the disasters themselves. What other factors are there? In the developing world, where most disasters occur, there appear to be three major causes which dominate disaster processes:

* human vulnerability resulting from poverty and inequality;
* environmental degradation owing to poor land use; and
* rapid population growth, especially among the poor.

Disasters and the poor

When one compares the number of people killed per disaster against the income of the country involved (see Figure 7), one finds a steep rise in mortality with decreasing income. There are over 3,000 deaths per disaster in low-income countries, and less than 500 per event in high-income countries.

Confusion in definitions causes debate about the numbers of disasters affecting various countries. British geographer Phil O'Keefe finds most disasters in poor countries, few in middle-income nations, and many disasters (due to ''property damage'' definitions) in wealthy countries (see Figure 8). Gunnar Hagman of the Swedish Red Cross finds evidence that most disaster victims are found in poor countries, most disasters are found in middle-income countries, and most property damage is caused in the rich nations. He speculates that the middle-income nations may have the most disaster events because of an aggressive economic development policy which includes overcultivation, deforestation and other forms of environmental degradation.

However, while some developed nations may be as prone to disasters as poor nations, the people of wealthier nations are not as vulnerable to disasters; they do not die in as large numbers.

Both Tokyo, Japan, and Managua, Nicaragua, are prone to earthquakes. But the people of Tokyo are far less vulnerable to injury by earthquake because Tokyo has strictly enforced building codes, zoning regulations and earthquake training and communications systems. In Managua, there are still many people living in top-heavy, mud-brick houses on hillsides. They are vulnerable.

	Number of disaster events 1960-1981	Number of people killed
Low-income economy		
Afghanistan	12	540
Bangladesh	63	633,000
Burma	26	1,500
Chad	14	2,300
China	20	247,000
Ethiopia	16	103,000
Gambia	11	200
Haiti	17	6,400
India	96	60,000
Laos	11	400
Madagascar	13	420
Mali	13	540
Mozambique	13	1,100
Nepal	19	2,900
Niger	12	320
Pakistan	21	7,400
Somalia	11	19,000
Sri Lanka	18	1,900
Sudan	11	310
Tanzania	12	590
Upper Volta	16	870
Vietnam	22	8,800
Middle-income economy		
Algeria	20	3,800
Argentina	17	650
Bolivia	21	530
Brazil	39	4,100
Chile	17	8,000
Colombia	26	1,800
Costa Rica	16	70
Dominican Rep.	10	3,300
Ecuador	21	640
Greece	15	190
Honduras	13	8,400
Hong Kong	10	680
Indonesia	59	17,000
Iran	38	48,000
Malaysia	10	310
Mauritius	11	20
Mexico	37	2,600
Morocco	18	13,000
Nicaragua	17	106,000
Panama	11	100
Peru	31	91,000
Philippines	76	17,000
Senegal	16	70
South Africa	11	830
South Korea	27	2,900
Thailand	10	1,300
Turkey	33	12,000
Yugoslavia	14	1,500
High-income economy		
Italy	24	6,100
Japan	43	2,700
Spain	12	1,900

Figure 9. The biggest losses of life from disasters are in poor and middle-income countries (by World Bank definitions). (Source: Prevention Better than Cure, Swedish Red Cross, 1984, based on League of Red Cross and USOFDA statistics.)

This difference is shown by a list of disaster events and fatalities over 1960-81 (Figure 9). Japan suffered 43 earthquakes and other disasters and lost 2,700 people: 63 deaths per disaster. Peru suffered 31 disasters with 91,000 dead: 2,900 dead per disaster.

Bindi V. Shah of the London School of Economics in 1983 published a global survey of disasters between 1947 and 1980, using a definition similar to that of the Natural Hazard Research Group. She found that both the frequency of disasters and number of people killed have been increasing in all "sudden impact" disasters since 1976. (She did not deal with the main slow onset disaster, drought.) She too found that death tolls were highest in the poorest, least developed nations. She concluded: "World population pressure and hunger for land are forcing more and more people to inhabit the earth's hazardous zones. It is not major changes in the earth's climate and structure that have led to an increase in disasters, but the concentration of social and economic activity in disaster-prone areas."

Shah's analysis is fine as far as it goes. But it deals only with human vulnerability. It does not explain how people can alter their environment to cause more frequent and more deadly disasters.

The environment

The poor countries which suffer such disastrous disasters are the same countries in which environmental degradation is proceeding most rapidly. Countries with severe deforestation, erosion, overcultivation and overgrazing tend to be hardest hit by disasters.

Does environmental degradation play a role in causing disasters? Science first studied disaster trigger mechanisms: climatological and geological processes. It then looked at how people behave in disasters. It has relatively recently begun to consider how humans can organise against disasters. Only in the last few years have a few scientists begun to catalogue the many ways in which humans can make "natural" disasters more frequent and more dangerous.

These ways fall into two broad categories. First, people can alter their environment to make it more *prone* to certain disaster triggers, mainly to drought and flood. Second, people (and it appears from fatality statistics to be mainly poor people) can live in dangerous structures on dangerous ground, making themselves more exposed and *vulnerable* to disaster trigger mechanisms.

A flood is too much water. Humans can make land prone to flooding by removing the trees and other vegetation which absorb this water.

A drought is too little water. Humans can make land more drought-prone by removing the vegetation and soil systems which absorb and store water in ways that are beneficial to humans.

If there is any truth in the idea that people are actually altering their environment to cause more floods and droughts, then one would expect to find these disaster categories affecting more and more people and their numbers increasing rapidly. They are. As indicated by the above statistics of Gunnar Hagman, floods are increasing fastest in frequency and in number of people affected, while droughts affect the largest number of people and are also affecting a great many more each decade.

In other disasters, such as cyclones and tsunamis, humans can increase their vulnerability by removing bits of their natural environment which may act as buffers to these extreme natural forces. Such acts include destroying reefs, cutting mangrove forests and clearing inland forests.

People can make themselves more exposed to disasters. The rich may be as guilty of this as the poor. A Caribbean island developer who erects a luxury hotel on a recently filled seafront, newly exposed to the force of the waves by the removal of a reef, is placing his guests at risk from hurricanes and earthquakes, both relatively common hazards in the region.

But such cases are rare compared to the plight of the poor. In many cities of the Third World, the poor live on land prone to floods, mudslides and avalanches during earthquakes. They live in self-built shelters unable to stand up to strong wind, rain or tremors. They are not taught or advised how to protect themselves from natural disasters.

Disaster prevention measures taken by the state —sea walls, terracing, levees (dykes along the river bank) — tend not to affect the poor. Such measures raise the value of property they protect; the poor cannot afford to live on land of any great value. The poor can afford only dangerous or unhealthy land. The poorest in the slums of Rio de Janeiro live on steep slopes which often wash from under them. The poor of Guatemala City and suburbs are tossed down the slopes on which they live with every earthquake. Millions of Bangladesh's poorest live on a river delta prone to cyclones and floods.

If one adapts a definition of disaster based upon amount of property damage and number of lives lost, then poverty is as much a cause of an "earthquake disaster" as the movements of the earth. Deforestation is as much a cause of a "flood disaster" as rainfall.

These relatively new ideas raise questions for the various groups interested in disasters:

* For governments: Can a government be more effective in protecting its people from flooding by working to change patterns of forest clearance?
* For relief, aid and volunteer agencies active in disasters: Might it make more sense to invest some effort and funds in development before a disaster occurs, rather than putting all investments in relief efforts after the event?
* For journalists: Is it enough to merely count the dead and describe the

Mark Edwards/Earthscan

Deforestation in Nepal makes both homes and elaborately terraced fields vulnerable to floods when monsoon rains, unimpeded by vegetation, roar down the southern slopes of the Himalayas. Recent years have seen many more floods, but no more rain.

damage? Or is it a journalist's job to look behind the scenes of destruction to expose ways in which people, politics and social systems have been responsible for any given disaster?

* For those responsible for development: Are they putting too much emphasis on "growth at any price", a policy which may leave more and more people on the margins of society, dangerously exposed to disasters?

These questions will be considered again in Chapter Eight.

Chapter 2

Droughts: too little water

"This damn drought wouldna' been half so bad if it hadna' come
smack in the middle of a dry spell!"
Attributed to US Midwestern farmer, 1983

Ari Toubo Eibrahim, Niger's Minister of Agriculture, told an audience of foreign journalists in 1982 that his ministry had done away with all Western scientific definitions of drought which depended on measuring quantities of rainfall. It now uses another definition: "Not as much water as the people need".

This may be somewhat imprecise, but in fact it represents a new way of looking at drought which could be helpful to agricultural and soil scientists. To a farmer, a drought is not necessarily about rainfall.

In the Caribbean, earthquakes, volcanoes and hurricanes are the most dramatic natural hazards. But drought and wind erosion cause more damage and economic loss. The Windward Islands — Dominica, Grenada, St Lucia and St Vincent — tend to slope steeply from the tops of peaks to the beaches. Bananas are the most important export, accounting for more than 70% of St Lucia's total agricultural exports.

The bananas are cultivated on lower hillslopes, which have variable rainfall. The unprotected topsoil beneath the trees is washed away by rain erosion and blown away by the wind. There is little topsoil to retain rainwater, so the rain which falls immediately moves down the slopes and away from the crops. In some areas, old channels built to remove water from former sugarcane fields help carry the water away from the bananas.

In such conditions, the only meaningful measure of rainfall is on a day by day basis. Between 1970 and 1975, over $20 million in banana producer revenues was lost due to "daily" drought conditions, even in the middle of the rainy season. Thus a crop can be damaged by "drought" in the midst of a better than average rainy season.

Scientists have observed the same effect in Haiti, where deforestation has led to catastrophic erosion. Rains may come, but the water runs quickly down the bare slopes, and the crops do not get the benefit. The plants have all the symptoms of drought-affliction. Botanist Jack Ewel of the University of Florida has called this condition "pseudo-drought", but the only way to

A Somali woman digs for water in a river bed. Even in the worst drought, some water is available. Simple technologies such as micro-catchments and low stone dams in river beds can make more of this water available for crops.

tell it from a "real" drought is by measuring the rainfall. To the farmer, the effect is exactly the same.

The Cagayan River valley in the north of Luzon island in the Philippines has undergone thorough study by the International Rice Research Institute (IRRI) of the Philippines, which is trying to develop a successful rice variety to flourish without irrigation there. The government started a large-scale irrigation project in the area, but abandoned it because it proved too expensive to keep up flows of water. The local people practice slash-and-burn agriculture, but do not allow time for adequate regeneration. This has led to erosion and loss of topsoil.

Lack of vegetation and topsoil means that the land cannot retain the water. The old irrigation channels actually take water away from the crops. So normal rains become "floods", and these are followed quickly by "droughts". And all of this can happen in years of normal average rainfall. After several years work, the IRRI has been unable to produce a rice strain that can flourish when drought follows quickly on the heels of total submersion.

These "droughts" during plentiful rainfall — with the damage to crops associated with seasons of little rain — make nonsense of the three types of drought defined by geographers:

* "precipitation drought" due to lack of rainfall;
* "runoff drought" due to low levels of river flow; and
* "aquifer drought" due to a lack of groundwater.

In fact, US disaster expert I. Burton defines drought in Tanzania not in terms of rainfall, but in terms of crop production. A "major" drought is one that diminishes crop yields by as much as 30% and a "severe" drought would "cause a loss of crop and animal production of about 8%". This definition not only removes drought from a measurement of rain but emphasises how narrow the margins are in Third World agriculture.

Rain, soil, drought and climate

When US climatologist C.W. Thornthwaite measured average monthly rainfall for Lagos, Sokoto (in northern Nigeria on the southern border of the Sahel region) and London, he found that Sokoto receives 100 mm (4 inches) more rain a year than London. But most of Sokoto's rain comes in July, August and September. There are five months during which Sokoto receives no rain at all. London's rain is evenly spread throughout the year.

The Sahel's rains come during a few months —when they come at all — and during those months it often comes in downpours. Most of the tropics, whether rainy or arid, gets its rain in seasons of intense rainfall between dry seasons. For these rains to do crops any good, the soil must retain water.

Yet most of Africa's soil is infertile sand and laterite soils (with a high content of iron and aluminium compounds, which become hard on exposure to sun and air). Sand and laterite not only erode easily, but hold little water compared to the clayey and humus-rich soils of the temperate zones. Laterite soils, when devegetated and exposed to sun and rain, can bake into a hard, concrete-like texture which is almost impossible to cultivate and absorbs virtually no rainfall. Soils throughout the tropics generally tend to be poorer than temperate soils. There are, however, many exceptions, such as the volcanic soils of Indonesia and Burundi, the deep clays of the northeast coast of Brazil, the Gezira area of Sudan and south of Lake Chad.

In the tropics, soils naturally prone to erosion receive a harder buffeting by rainstorms. At a rainfall rate of 35 mm (1.4 ins) per hour, there is a sharp rise in rain's ability to cause "splash erosion": to knock crumbs of soil loose, beginning the process of wash erosion that cuts deep into the soil.

Vegetation helps fragile tropical soils to retain water. When this vegetation is removed, topsoil rapidly erodes, according to Dr W.E. Ormerod of the London School of Hygiene and Tropical Medicine (who assembled most of the above data on Sahel rainfall and soil).

Areas with widespread erosion are more prone to drought — because the soils can retain less and less water —and more prone to floods for the same reason.

The big droughts

But surely the major droughts of several years affecting several nations are due plainly and simply to lack of rain?

In early 1984, more than 150 million people in 24 western, eastern and southern African nations were "on the brink of starvation" because of droughts, and "famine has already caused deaths in some countries", according to a UN Food and Agriculture Organization (FAO) report. In October 1983, FAO had launched a general alert concerning the food situation in Africa.

Rains in 1983-84 either did not come, or came too little, too early or too late. Countries outside the Sahel were also affected:

* Ethiopia: in four northern regions five million people were suffering after several consecutive years of drought. Eritrea had little rain except on the coast. Civil war also disrupted agriculture and food distribution schemes.
* Sudan: Eastern Sudan had a poor harvest, but refugees from Ethiopia continued to pour in. The British relief organisation OXFAM reported that in one camp the new arrivals were not fleeing war, but were drought

Y. Muller/FAO

A Gambian farmer in his millet field, destroyed by the 1984 droughts.
Overgrazing, overcultivation of fragile land and deforestation made the droughts
affecting 24 African nations in 1984 much more punishing than they need have
been.

refugees — farmers from Tigre and Wollo regions who were
malnourished upon arrival.

* Mozambique: Central and southern areas had had little or no rain since
1979, and with drought affecting the entire region many of the rivers
normally flowing into the country had dried up. The government
reported in late 1983 that "for the rural population in many areas the
only food supply during the last months were some fruits and leaves
growing in the savannah forest". A UN report in early 1984 said 10,000
people had already died in three of the worst hit provinces and at least
750,000 people were in need of urgent aid.

* Zimbabwe: All eight districts got some rain in late 1983, but the water
supply remained critical, with cattle dying in some areas. Living cattle
were weak, so in some areas there was no draught power, causing people
to use hoes to plough, reducing the area they could plant and so
affecting future harvests.

The weather was clearly to blame. But in each nation human activity made the disaster worse:

* Ethiopia: Robert Lamb of UNEP reported that "the highlands, especially the regions of Wollo, Tigre and Gondor have been so overfarmed, overgrazed and deforested that efforts to scrape a bare living from this land threaten to destroy it permanently. The erosion resulting from overuse causes the Ethiopian highlands to lose one billion tonnes of topsoil each year, according to UN estimates." The situation is so desperate that the government has begun a major resettlement scheme to transfer farmers from the highlands to underpopulated lowlands. Government officials have referred to the people to be moved as "environmental refugees".

* Sudan: For some time the Sahara has been encroaching upon the Sudan across a broad front at a rate of about five kilometres (3 miles) a year, claimed Sudanese President Jaafar Mohamed Al Nimeri in late 1983 at the FAO annual conference. In fact, scientists say that the process of desertification is less like the advance of a wall of sand than the outbreak of a blotchy skin disease, here and there over an area of 100-200 sq km (60-125 sq miles). Yet the Sudanese government continues to allow, even to encourage, overcultivation and overgrazing in the afflicted areas. President Nimeri told the FAO meeting that the nation's motto was "agriculture and more agriculture".

* Mozambique: Some 8,000-10,000 Mozambique National Resistance Movement fighters, widely reported to be backed by South Africa, destroyed homes, state-run shops, health centres and crops in late 1983 and early 1984, according to OXFAM. They prevented government delivery of relief supplies, frightened people out of planting their crops and caused many to flee to safer areas, especially in the two southern-most provinces, Gaza and Inhambane. Mozambique has suffered both drought and destabilisation.

* Zimbabwe: As Zimbabwe approached independence in 1980, the whites — 5% of the population — controlled 50% of the land. Economic and security problems have meant that land redistribution since then has been slow. African families crowded onto poor quality "tribal lands" have been forced to overcultivate and deforest these fragile areas. Poor rainfall has been the final blow. The cattle-herding Ndebele people do not feel they are getting their fair share of the redistributed land under the Shona-dominated government of Premier Mugabe. Their own land has been overgrazed by their herds, and the Ndebele appeared to be suffering the worst from the drought.

An FAO report released in July 1984 listed six African countries which would face severe food shortages right through 1985, due to the failures of three successive harvests. Zimbabwe and Mozambique were joined on the list by Angola, Botswana, Lesotho and Zambia.

The Sahel: 1968-73

The 1968-73 Sahel drought, which most directly affected Chad, Mali, Mauritania, Niger, Senegal and Upper Volta (now called Burkina-Faso), was made worse by human action and inaction. According to a report to the 1977 UN Conference on Desertification (UNCOD), between 100,000 and 150,000 died in the region. And in a report by the Club du Sahel (an informal collection of countries giving aid to the region) and the Permanent Interstate Committee for Drought Control in the Region (CILSS — an organisation of Sahelian governments) the toll was 50,000-100,000.

But the death toll tells little of the story. Jean Copans of the Centre for African Studies in Paris, claims that by 1974 there were 200,000 people in Niger (5% of the population) completely dependent on food distribution; 250,000 people in Mauritania (20% of the population) had moved to towns and were completely destitute; and in Mali another 250,000 people (5%) were totally dependent on aid in towns.

The drought focused scientific and public attention on the Sahel in particular, and on the climate in general. Scientists checked to see if climatic change was to blame.

"No serious analysis of the available data is known to show a falling trend of rainfall in the zone over the period for which records are available", concluded E.G. Davy in a report for the UN World Meteorological Organization; his findings also covered arid zones in India and the Middle East. Other climatologists agreed. Rainfall has been lower over the past 15-20 years than during the 1950s and early 1960s, but there is no evidence that this represents a major climate change. Scientists also looked at the historical record and found that rains have often failed in the Sahel. The nomadic Tuareg tribespeople have given earlier droughts names like "Forget your wife" and "The sale of children".

Alan Grainger of Oxford University, UK wrote in a 1982 Earthscan report:

"Drought triggers a crisis, but does not cause it. Overcultivation and overgrazing weaken the land, allowing no margin when drought arrives. The high human pressure will continue during the drought, leading ultimately to even greater and more visible damage to the land and the deaths of large numbers of animals."

After the drought, both the Club du Sahel and CILSS agreed that food self-sufficiency was the main goal of national and regional development. Over

1975-80, donor countries committed $7.5 billion in aid. Yet only 24% of this was actually directed toward agriculture, and less than 40% of all agriculture and forestry projects were rural. The rest went to urban-based support projects. Of the $7.5 billion, only 8% went for cropping which depends on rain rather than irrigation. (Some 28% of all agricultural aid went to cash crops, most of which were exported. In 1960-70, almost all aid to "rainfed" cropping went to cotton and peanut projects.) Only 5% of the $7.5 billion went to livestock raising, a major activity in the region. Only 1.4% of aid went to forestry/ecology in 1980, up from 0.35% in 1975. Writing in 1983 of the ways in which both aid-giving and aid-receiving nations had been spending money to combat desertification, Dr Harold Dregne of Texas Tech University (US), noted:

> "Governments do not see desertification as a high-priority item. Rangeland deterioration, accelerated soil erosion and salinisation and waterlogging do not command attention until they become crisis items. Lip service is paid to combating desertification, but the political will is directed elsewhere. There seems to be little appreciation that a major goal of many developing nations, that of food self-sufficiency, cannot be attained if soil and plant resources are allowed to deteriorate."

Each year the region falls further and further behind its goal of food self-sufficiency. Population is increasing at the rate of 2.5% a year and cereal production rises at 1% a year. Between 1955 and 1979, the land area under millet and sorghum increased at an average rate of 3.4% per year, but production rose only 2.5% per year. Thus yields per hectare are falling. Food aid to the region never falls below 100,000 tonnes a year.

Why, when everyone seems agreed that food self-sufficiency is of utmost importance for the Sahel, does so little money go to agriculture?

First, the peasants who live in arid lands have little political power. The governments — civil servants, police, army — are in the capitals. So leaders like to keep aid in the capitals — whether it be food aid or the construction of buildings and other projects which generate employment.

Second, for the same political reasons, Sahelian governments have a policy of providing cheap food to urban centres. So subsistence farmers rarely produce extra food to sell in the market — because the selling price does not pay for the fertiliser or better seed they need to increase production.

Third, the donor nations have few experts who can increase yields of sorghum and millet in arid lands, but do have experts at constructing roads and buildings, and they have companies manufacturing equipment for such purposes.

Yield per hectare of foods is falling because increasing populations tend to push farmers and herders onto marginal lands, and because plantations

Mark Edwards/Earthscan

A mixed herd of cattle and sheep in Niger. Surrounded by drought-stricken nations in 1984, Niger produced a foods surplus, partly by encouraging herders to sell excess animals.

of cash crops get the best land along southern rivers, pushing subsistence farmers and nomads north toward the desert.

Fourth, livestock numbers are climbing toward their pre-drought (1968) levels. The contribution of domestic animals to desertification is a controversial issue, but overgrazing is certainly playing a role in degrading land in the Sahel. In 1980, the numbers of cows and sheep in the Sahel were at 70% of their pre-drought levels; the numbers of goats, horses and donkeys, were equal to 1968 levels, according to a UNDP report.

"The situation has become extremely precarious in the Sudan, as in all countries in the region, and is today much more delicate than in the late 1960s. The next serious drought might well entail more severe consequences than the last one", predicted French rangeland expert Michel Baumer in 1982.

"Whether you see the desert as advancing or the Sahel as losing ground, a real catastrophe is on the way", predicted Mamadou Mahamane, director of a Niger forestry aid project the same year.

The Sahel today

In 1983, rains were either too late or too little across much of the Sahel, except in the south.

In Mauritania, the rains failed in 1982 and 1983. The Mauritanian government distributed food in late 1983, but this went to centres up to 100 km (60 miles) away from some villages. There was a mass migration to the capital Nouakchott, which already contained half the country's population.

In Burkina-Faso (fomerly called Upper Volta), there was almost no 1983 harvest in the north. Waterholes were only a quarter full. An aid worker in Oudalan reported that peasants there were as badly off as in 1972.

All the Sahelian countries except Niger were on the FAO's list of threatened African countries. Niger also suffered from late 1983 rains, but its government has perhaps done more than any other Sahelian government to promote food self-sufficiency, emphasising food rather than cash crops after the 1968-73 drought. Niger seems to be the lead country in the region in terms of extending advice and services to the countryside. Its leaders took quick action in 1983, selling off 5,000 head of cattle from government farms as a warning to pastoralists that grazing lands would not be sufficient for several months. It advised herders to move to better pastures and began to provide animal fodder to help get the herds through the 1983-84 dry season.

Latin America

Though current droughts may seem a uniquely African scourge, they also regularly hit Asia and Latin America.

Northeast Brazil, an area roughly the size of Europe, has a few very rich planters who own vast sugarcane plantations and many very poor peasants who own little or no land. It was in its fifth year of drought in 1983; some 20 million people were affected. In some areas, 90% of the 1983 harvest was lost and people were reduced to eating lizards and cacti.

But here too, the problem was not only rain. "The drought in the Northeast is a creeping, not a sudden disaster", reported OXFAM. "Irregular and inadequate rainfall has been slowly and insidiously destroying peasant agriculture which has already been undermined by a grossly inequitable land tenure system." (See below: "Brazil: the poor pay for disasters".)

In the high valleys of Bolivia and southern Peru, over two million people had little food after the almost complete failure of the 1983 potato crop. It was Bolivia's worst natural disaster in more than a century. (The nation's eastern lowlands were flooded in March 1983, and some 40,500 hectares (100,000 acres) of prime agricultural land was destroyed.)

There was rain in the area toward the end of 1983. But as it came late, 1984 was also expected to be a bad year, and observers estimated it could take four years to overcome the effects of the 1983 drought.

Some 20% of the land area of Latin America is either affected or likely to be affected by desertification, according to data prepared for a UN world map of desertification (1977). Maximum threats are in Chile, Argentina, Mexico and Peru. Among the Andes nations, according to the *Arid Lands Newsletter* (US): Bolivia is 15% arid, 10% semi-arid; Ecuador is 5% semi-arid; Peru is 20% arid; Venezuela is 5% semi-arid.

Bolivia is one of the least developed nations in the region. Children have a life expectancy at birth of 49 years, compared to a tropical Latin American average of 62; 131 of every thousand infants die before their first birthday, compared to an average in tropical Latin America of 74 per thousand. The nation has a per capita GNP of $570, less than one third of the average of $1,890 for tropical South America.

The country is sparsely populated, but as only 3% of the land is arable and as the rural people are especially poor, most peasants intensively farm small plots of poor soil. Fallow periods become shorter every year, according to OXFAM. "There are droughts in a few departments each year. But in 1983 drought stretched throughout the high valleys", they said.

In mid-1983, the Bolivian army announced that it would cultivate 607,000 hectares (1.5 million acres) of land it owned to offset potato shortages. But the fact that the army kept that much arable land out of circulation was regarded by some local relief workers as an indication of how lightly the government takes the plight of the rural smallholders.

As noted in Chapter Three, most of the cultivated soil in the Andes suffers erosion. Only 2.7% of Peru is classified as "arable", but according to Peruvian forester Marc Dourojeanni, 30% of that nation's territory is affected by water erosion, both on the arid western slopes, and on the humid eastern slopes, to which much of the agriculture is now moving.

The populations of the Andean countries of Bolivia, Ecuador and Peru are all growing faster than the regional averages. As these populations seek more farmland, more land will become more prone to drought.

The Indian subcontinent

India has been more affected by drought and associated famine than any other country in the world. Floods in the heavily populated northern, eastern and coastal zones often make headlines, but over 80% of the subcontinent is chronically drought-prone. In fact, 1983 was the first year that Africa had more drought victims than India. Even in that year, when drought affected 150 million Africans, 120 million Indians were suffering from less well-publicised droughts.

The subcontinent has suffered at least a dozen great famines in which a million or more people have died in the past 1,000 years; there have been four major famines in the past 100 years.

L.A. Ramdas, an Indian geographer, reckoned in 1949 that the subcontinent was liable to a subcontinent-wide drought once every 20 years, but to drought in one or more provinces in one year out of every five. He estimated that widespread favourable conditions — neither drought nor flood — could only be expected in one year out of every two.

The 1967-68 drought-related crop failures caused relatively little suffering, while the 1972-73 drought may have left as many as one million people dead of starvation, according to Canadian geographer Kenneth Hewitt, who wondered why the two very similar disasters should have had such different effects.

In 1967-68, the United States had good harvests and no major foreign bidders for its grain; there were no other major shortage disasters beside the one which occurred in India. India's grain production was down 19% over the previous year in 1966-67, but in those two years approximately 20% of the US wheat crop was shipped to India, on fairly favourable terms, according to Hewitt.

In 1972-73, drought again hit the southern and northwestern areas of the Indian subcontinent. But this time: both China and the Soviet Union had suffered bad harvests and put in bids for US grain; the Nixon administration, embattled by the Watergate scandal, was willing to sell to the highest bidder; industrialised nations had just recognised the seriousness of the Sahel drought, and were sending aid in that direction; India was hit by the sharply rising oil prices of the period, and could not afford grain; and India and Pakistan were embroiled in the Bangladesh secession.

"Human institutions that could have been used to avert famine were turning out to be no more reliable than the monsoon", wrote Hewitt. Political and other events outside India turned the drought into a major human disaster.

Induced "droughts": US and USSR

It is not only the peasants in poor tropical countries who can help cause drought conditions on land which previously provided thousands of people with a living. It can happen in both capitalist and communist societies of the North.

During the First World War, rapidly rising wheat prices encouraged US farmers to plough up the prairie grasses of the western Great Plains to plant wheat. The droughts of the early 1930s ruined many of these farmers and turned the area into what was then called "the Dust Bowl". Photos show mounds of sand and sandstorms which would never have occurred if the prairie grass and its tough root system had been left in place.

The US government responded with massive soil conservation and rehabilitation programmes, as many farmers migrated westwards to California. But as US environmentalist Erik Eckholm wrote in *Down to Earth* (Pluto Press; Norton, 1982): "Tens of millions in the Third World today have no California to head for when the soils that sustain them blow away." Few Third World governments have effective soil conservation programmes either.

In the 1950s, the Soviet Union began a "virgin land programme" as part of a national effort to increase grain production. Millions of hectares of the semi-arid Kazakh Steppes in Soviet Central Asia were ploughed and planted with cereals. Soviet soil scientists slowly realised that they were creating a desert by state decree. By 1965, most of the work had been halted; some of the land was allowed to return to grass, and anti-erosion measures — windbreaks, increased fallow periods and the use of machinery which leaves crop stubble in the fields — were taken on other stretches.

Yet at least three million hectares (7.4 million acres) still suffer severe erosion, and during dry spells sandstorms are a problem where there were none before.

US droughts: spreading the risk

While much of Africa and parts of Latin America and Asia were suffering droughts in 1983, the United States suffered a combination of heatwave and drought from the eastern states to Texas. The drought coincided with the Reagan administration's "payment-in-kind" (PIK) programme, which encouraged farmers not to plant and paid them in crops — corn, wheat, rice or cotton — for land not planted.

PIK was an effort to lower US grain reserves. In the late summer of 1983, officials were estimating that PIK had reduced the potential corn crop by 2.2 billion bushels and the drought had done away with another one billion bushels. Farmers who bet on PIK did well; many of those who planted anyway suffered badly.

But US farmers suffer less in a drought than do Sahelian farmers, mainly because of the vast amounts of government help they get. In 1983, for the first time in US history, the government spent more supporting farmers (over $20 billion), than the nation's total net farm income, according to US environmental writer David Sheridan.

Since the 1890s, there have been four major droughts in the US Great Plains, one about every 20 years: in the 1890s, 1910s, 1930s and 1950s, according to Richard Warrick of the Natural Hazards Information Center, University of Colorado, US. There were less severe droughts in the 1870s and 1970s and during the summer of 1983.

During the 1890s, there were widespread reports of starvation deaths and malnutrition in the drought-afflicted central and southern High Plains. There were similar reports during the 1910 drought from the Dakotas and eastern Montana. There was little relief effort or even the admission of a problem in either case, because the state governments were trying to lure in settlers by promoting the region as prosperous farmland.

Over the decades, human suffering has diminished from drought to drought in the US, largely because of state and federal programmes such as the Federal Crop Insurance Corporation, the Soil Conservation Service and the Agricultural Stabilization and Conservation Service.

These organisations, working with increasing numbers of highly educated farmers, introduced schemes to conserve water and protect its sources (evaporation control, seepage reduction, etc); and to protect farmland (contouring, terracing, leaving fields fallow in summer, ploughing stubble back into the fields, drought-resistant crops and varieties, flexible cropping plans and land use regulations). Crop insurance, reserves of feed and grain and various types of financial reserves (including reasonable credit) add to security during drought. Between the 1930s and the late 1970s, the Great Plains also experienced a sixfold increase in irrigation.

According to Warrick, all of this has resulted in a shifting of the impact of droughts to higher levels. The harsh realities of starvation and migration facing the 1890s farmer, he says, were replaced locally during the 1950s "by the hardships of paying insurance premiums, by slightly premature retirements and by a lingering uneasiness over receiving government support. The national obligation to bail out the Plains farmer shifts much of the stress to the US citizen. This stress takes the form of increased taxation and of rising prices for scarce agricultural commodites."

But Warrick warns that the security of the US Great Plains farmer has been achieved through "an increasing commitment to greater social organisation and technological sophistication". It is a complex, very expensive structure. In a really severe drought, "the failure of these mechanisms under severe stress might result in far-ranging, unexpected disruptive consequences".

The Sahelian states are hardly in a position to mimic the details of the Great Plains agricultural system. But there are inexpensive technologies for water and cropland conservation and protection which are not getting to the Sahelian subsistence farmers because — as detailed above — little government and foreign aid ever reaches these farmers. The basic concept of spreading the burden of disaster throughout the population has not yet been adopted in the Sahel or other drought-prone Third World areas. The Sahelian cities are artificially supported by food aid, most of which goes to governments and is used to keep urban elites content.

Instead of allowing the prices of agricultural products to rise to help pay for agricultural security and improvements, as in the US, Sahelian governments keep these artificially low to maintain stability and to buy loyalty in cities. Tax revenue does not get to the countryside, but stays in the cities, for the same reason.

Warrick's warning against dependency on technological sophistication and social organisation is even more important for such a delicate area as the Sahel. Many of the "big ideas" tried in the Sahel — massive irrigation projects, reorganisation of pastoral life and the settling of nomads — have failed.

The Sahelian nations lack the technology for big technical fixes, and do not know enough about how their rural societies operate to reorganise them effectively. Improvement in the Sahel will come, experts believe, only when the states find ways to make their farmers more secure and their efforts more profitable. This is also the way improvement began on the US Great Plains.

Brazil: the poor pay for disasters

The drought in northeastern Brazil, which entered its sixth year in early 1984, offers an example of a system for coping with drought which places most of the burden on the poorest, and in some cases even makes the rich better off. (Much of the information in this section comes from relief workers in the area who did not wish to be quoted.)

The 19th century Brazilian Emperor Dom Pedro II pledged that no jewel would remain in his crown while the Northeast suffered drought. Today his crown is in a museum in southern Brazil, all its jewels in place.

This century the Northeast has suffered 17 droughts, and in 1978 the Aerospace Centre in São Jose dos Campos warned the government of a seven-year drought (the basis of this prediction was not clear). There were some rains in late 1983, but residents still expected two more years of drought.

There are no reliable statistics on deaths and malnutrition in the nine states affected. In Pernambuco state alone some 45,000 people have died as the result of the five years of drought, according to the Federation of Rural Workers Unions of that state. One official estimate holds that three million poor people may die as direct and indirect results of the current drought.

"Foreign aid experts here are comparing the harm done to human life and nature with that caused by the current great drought in sub-Saharan Africa", said a report in the New York Times newspaper in late March 1984. It added that 25 million of the more than 30 million people in the area were affected, with 15 million suffering directly from hunger and thirst.

The New York Times quoted Valfrido Salmito, co-ordinator of the nation's relief effort, explaining why Brazil was not accepting major outside aid: "It is humiliating to ask for food. It's an embarrassing situation because Brazil is the fourth largest producer of grains in the world."

The hunger is the result of "a man-made drought, a fact which has been stressed by church and social agencies working with the poor", according to Christian Aid Magazine. "Years of government mismanagement has seen large funds which should have gone to provide work and social reform for the poor allocated instead into bolstering the fortunes of large landowners and private industry.''

The Brazilian government also tends toward either grand projects or schemes which attack symptoms but not the disease, according to local relief workers. Mario Andreazza, transport minister in the 1960s, advocated sending the poor ''nordestinos'' (northeasterners) to colonise the Amazon. This ended in disaster and extreme suffering among the colonists, and today large-scale ranching and logging industries have taken over in the Amazon. Andreazza, now interior minister, advocates a $2-3 billion project to use the water of the Tocantins and Sao Francisco Rivers to irrigate the Northeast.

Symptom-attacking schemes have enriched many people and given rise to what some locals call the ''Industria da Seca'' (drought industry). Among these was the building of a series of dams in Pernambuco despite warnings of flash floods by residents; floods washed away all of the dams.

Since 1979, the government has disbursed over $500 million for ''Emergency Work Fronts'', reaching about two million drought victims by the end of 1983. These schemes pay unemployed rural workers or smallholders to help supplement lost income. Groups of 15-60 men work to deepen reservoirs, build earth barrages and clear land for when the rains finally come.

Yet most of this work — administered by the Brazilian national drought relief agency DNOCS, the army and the government agricultural extension agency EMATER — is done on the property of large landowners, helping the rich through the drought and making them better prepared for when it ends. The smallholders often find themselves building earth barrages to hold water on the land of the rich and keep it away from their own smallholdings.

Brazilian Vice-President Aureliano Chaves visited the Northeast in August 1983 and promised a further $18 million. Yet much of this was to go to companies and ''infrastructure'' projects; only a third was for direct emergency relief. Meanwhile, the state government of Ceara was asking for nearly $3 million just for one month's payments of the Emergency Work Fronts.

The government development agency for the Northeast, SUDENE, delivers water by tanker trucks; in the state of Rio Grande do Norte, water comes 130 km (80 miles) by train before 240 tankers take it to 130 cities and towns. Oil drums, tins and clay pots line the roads awaiting water trucks.

But truck routes are determined by local governments, often affected by local political interests. So large landowners may get daily deliveries. The fortunate poor along the routes to the big estates may get regular service, and those less fortunate may see a tanker every two weeks. Some landowners are conserving water by stopping their tenants and share-croppers from building their own wells and small dams, making them dependent on tanker deliveries to the landowners.

The Rural Workers Unions — while campaigning for simple things like time off for the Work Front workers to prepare their own land for when the drought ends — are also working for land reform. Hunger seems to be becoming a political issue in Brazil, especially among the prosperous middle class of the south. Media coverage of the 1983 floods in the south helped focus attention on the disaster in the Northeast. Magazines and television launched appeals for disaster victims, but the drought appeal raised less than the one for the flood victims of the prosperous south.

However, churches of the south were linking up with northeastern churches to channel money and materials, and such organisations as Rotary and Lions Clubs and the Red Cross were helping. These efforts might move Brazil toward spreading the disaster burden more evenly, and not letting the poor bear the brunt.

Drought and famine

Just as poor rainfall is not the single and direct cause of drought, drought is not the single and direct cause of famine.

People do not starve in a drought-related famine simply because there is no food. No relief worker has starved to death during a drought; no journalist has died of hunger while covering a drought. Because of a complex set of economic, cultural and political factors, these people are "entitled" to food, to borrow a concept from economist Amartya Sen. Due to economic, cultural and political reasons, the "victims" of the famine are not entitled to food.

Critics of this analysis point out that just because there is enough food available for journalists and relief workers to buy, does not necessarily mean there would be enough for all the hungry to buy if they had money.

The International Labour Organisation (ILO) studied the famines in Bengal in 1943, in Ethiopia in 1973 and in Bangladesh in 1974. It found that famine "chose" its victims by class and occupation, and there were many other factors at work besides food scarcity. In Bengal, food stocks were below the level of 1942 but were within the normal range of fluctuation. But wartime inflation had destroyed the Bengal currency. In Ethiopia, the lack of food was a highly localised phenomenon. But richer farmers had dismissed labourers and household staff because of low yields, so there were no wages to buy food. Dr John Rivers of the International Disaster Institute maintains that throughout the famine Ethiopia was a net exporter of food. In Bangladesh, there was actually more food available on a per person basis than in some recent non-famine years. But floods had disrupted industry and thus cut other employment opportunities.

In each case people's options were diminished. Those who suffered most were the landless labourers and the pastoralists who had to sell their livelihood — their cattle — to survive, at a time when there was no market for cattle.

B.M. Bhatia, in his 1967 study of Indian famines, also concluded that famine is not an imbalance between populations and natural resources, but that "instead of absolute want, famine under modern conditions has come to signify a sharp and abrupt rise in food prices which renders food beyond the reach of the poor who suffer starvation".

Flexibility and drought

Up to fairly recent times, people have relied on flexible responses to avoid the effects of droughts and other disasters.

The most basic form of flexibility is mobility, notes Canadian geographer Eric Waddell, who quotes an old Chinese proverb, "Of thirty ways to escape danger, running away is best".

Many of the coping mechanisms of the nomadic herdsmen of the Sahel depend on movement to another area, but there are also other ways of increasing flexibility. The Wodaabe Fulani people of Niger not only move seasonally (transhumance) from the southern cropped fields during the dry season to the northern Sahelian pastures as the rains begin in June, but move out of camps in different directions daily to seek water and grass. They carefully diversify their herds, mixing camels, sheep and goats with cows. Different animals have different needs for water and pasture and breed at different times, spreading risk. They trade their sheep, goats, hides, milk, butter and cheese with Hausa farmers for such staples as millet and sorghum. They rely on certain "fallback activities" such as short-term, spontaneous sedentarisation and wage labour. (The government has discouraged one traditional fallback activity: raiding other tribes.) They share animals in a very complex system of kinship duties and traditional exchanges. Animals may be given, loaned or rented out. A cow may be loaned until she has three calves; the borrower keeps the calves and returns the cow.

Flexibility can aid farmers as well as herders. New Guinea cultivators once moved into other areas during drought. But before doing so, they exhausted other possibilities. They typically planted gardens far apart and at different elevations, sowing crops resistant to various climate extremes — rain, drought, frost — in different gardens. (Chapter Seven describes how a government disaster relief programme virtually destroyed this flexible response system.)

Recently, a number of factors have virtually eliminated the flexibility of response of many marginal people in drought-prone areas. Most governments discourage "mobility" as a response to an emergency, and have also tried to settle nomads. Yet through custom, the herders still keep large numbers of animals. Population pressure — especially the growing numbers of cultivators — and government regulations such as grazing fees and range block systems also hinder mobility. Cultivators' flexibility is limited by their need to earn money by concentrating on perhaps only one cash crop. Also, their poverty and the lack of government agricultural extension means that

F. Botts/FAO

Drought-killed livestock beside the camp of Mali nomads. Few Sahelian governments give high priority to agriculture; resources go instead to keep urban elites happy. In Mali, more than 85% of the population makes its living off the land.

they have little or no choice in the varieties of subsistence crops which they plant. Investing all one's efforts in one variety of one staple is dangerous, especially in drought-prone areas.

US geographer Ben Wisner, studying ways used by traditional societies to diminish the effects of drought in Kenya in the past, found 157 different mechanisms at work, most of them complex sharing systems among extended families. Looking at the same society recently, he found only two of these mechanisms still at work: leaving the countryside for urban jobs, and prayer.

Flexibility today can cover a number of possibilities: the ability to move; a choice of types and varieties of cash and subsistence crops; a choice of markets for crops or livestock (in a drought, herders cannot sell their livestock locally because the bottom has dropped out of the market); alternative ways of making money, such as light industry; and government insurance schemes.

Flexibility is not only a defensive approach. Under the right conditions, it can even bring prosperity in drought-prone areas.

In the late 1920s a group of Mennonite Christians of German-Russian origin left Canada seeking cultural and religious freedom and settled in the remote "Chaco" region of Paraguay, some 750 km (465 miles) by small riverboat, rail and road from Asunción. Severe floods alternate with drought in this region of fine clayey and sandy soils.

Canadian geographers A. Hecht and J.W. Fretz, who studied three Mennonite settlements of almost 10,000 people, found that "in about one out of four years, major drought conditions exist in the Chaco". Yet after 50 years of hard struggle, these settlers, admittedly the offspring of immigrants with industrial and professional backgrounds, are flourishing.

They appear to succeed by spreading their options as widely as possible, planting cotton and castor beans as cash crops and peanuts, beans and sorghum as food crops. Harvests vary wildly from year to year; wheat proved so vulnerable to drought that the Mennonites ceased planting it in 1970. They have imported "buffalo grass" from Texas, which is an excellent cattle feed, does well on the Chaco soils and recuperates quickly after a drought. Milk from their cattle is turned into cheese and butter at their own dairy, thus providing a market for their milk, which they would not be able to sell as milk. A local tree provides a resin which is sold for use in perfumes and various industrial purposes.

Other local industries include a tannery, a shoe factory, a metal foundry, tile and brick yards, a furniture factory, a blacksmith and tinsmiths. The Paraguayan Mennonites have even set up an agriculture experiment station.

Such industries help the settlements survive drought years such as 1975, when harvests were only 48% of 1974 yields, in that the people can continue to produce things to sell. And today they also have supplies of saved capital upon which to draw.

Hecht and Fretz attribute the Mennonites' prosperity to "the ability to specialise in agricultural endeavours suitable to the environment" and the abandonment of unsuccessful crops attempted in the early years of the settlements. The authors draw from this the lesson that "environmentally sensitive regions are vulnerable when crop production strives to meet all needs", as in subsistence farming.

The Mennonites have moved beyond subsistence by overcoming great transport problems in getting products to markets, but more importantly by relying on a wide range of food and cash-producing options.

The cultivators of the Sahelian countryside lack agricultural options, markets which pay reasonable prices for any surpluses, and any manufacturing or industrial opportunities. The Mennonite experience offers the hope that well-considered tactics and economic development can offer at least the possibility of doing well amidst droughts.

Chapter 3

Floods

"Would that a lion had ravaged mankind
Rather than the flood."
(*Epic of Gilgamesh,* 3rd millenium BC)

A flood is too much water in the wrong place, whether it be an inundated city or a single street or field flooded due to a blocked drain. Among the trigger mechanisms are dam or levee failures; more rain than the landscape can dispose of; the torrential rains of hurricanes; tsunami; ocean storm surges; rapid snow melts; ice floes blocking a river; and burst water mains.

But most of the rapidly growing Third World flood disasters are caused by humans making their land more prone to floods and themselves more vulnerable.

Floods affect more people than any other disaster except droughts. But there are many more flood disasters than droughts, and the number affected by floods is increasing much more rapidly than those suffering droughts. According to figures from the US Office for Foreign Disaster Assistance (USOFDA), 18.5 million people per year were affected by droughts during the 1960s, and 24.4 million during the 1970s. Floods affected 5.2 million a year in the 1960s compared with 15.4 in the 1970s — an almost threefold increase. Over 1964-82, floods killed 80,000 people and affected 221 million worldwide.

In 1983 there were major floods in Bangladesh, China, India, Nepal and Papua New Guinea; there was also flooding in Argentina, Bolivia, Cuba, Ecuador, Paraguay and Peru. In 1983, the League of Red Cross and Red Crescent Societies launched eight international appeals to assist a total of 1.6 million flood victims in five Latin American nations.

Floods and forests

Until rain reaches the ground, humans have little influence over it. But whether water, once on the ground, becomes "a productive resource or a destructive hazard depends very largely on Man's management of vegetation and soils", according to a 1974 UNESCO report.

A key driving force in the yearly increase in flood disasters is the rapid

Mark Edwards/Earthscan

Haitian children bail out their house in a waterfront shantytown of Port-au-Prince, Haiti. The houses are flooded regularly both by high tides and rainfall running off eroded hills stripped of trees.

rate of deforestation in the tropics. According to an FAO/UNEP study in 1981, tropical forests are disappearing at the rate of 7.3 million hectares (18 million acres) per year: 4.2 million hectares (10.4 million acres) a year in Latin America; 1.8 million hectares (4.4 million acres) a year in Asia; and 1.3 million hectares (3.2 million acres) a year in Africa.

"In view of the likelihood that much of the vast area of the world's surface still forested will be deforested in coming decades, the consequence of this in leading to disastrous floods cannot be over-emphasised", wrote Professor L.D. Pryor in his 1982 report *Ecological Mismanagement in Natural Disasters* for the International Union for Conservation of Nature and Natural Resources (IUCN).

US environmentalist Erik Eckholm wrote in *Down to Earth* (Pluto Press; Norton, 1982): "Decades of research have proved that the deforestation of watersheds, especially around smaller rivers and streams, can increase the severity of flooding, reduce streamflows and dry up springs during dry seasons, and increase the load of sediment entering waterways. Yet most efforts to combat such problems have entailed engineering measures — dams, embankments, dredging — that address symptoms and not their causes. The exact contribution of deforestation to flood trends is probably impossible to pinpoint, but as flooding worsens in country after country, new attention is being given to watersheds.''

But the "decades of research" have not yielded consistent results. Reviewing the literature on watershed management and floods recently, Roy Ward, geographer at the University of Hull, UK, found that early this century soil conservationists believed that if one could only "stop the raindrop where it fell", one could minimise floods. By the middle of the 20th century, experts were pessimistic about the efficiency of managing land and its forests to control floods.

But "recent re-evaluation of the runoff process, together with more rigorous experimental work on the hydrological effects of land management techniques, have begun to revive cautious optimism", wrote Ward. Research done in the 1970s showed that "the felling of forest stands and the consequent reduction in evapo-transpiration (the combination of water uptake by plants and evaporation) alone can significantly increase flood volumes".

The effects can be quite dramatic. In the early 1970s, fire destroyed 265 sq km (102 sq miles) of forest in the catchment area of Wallace's Creek and the Yarrangobilly River in the Australian Alps. The flows of these streams and the amounts of soil they carried had been carefully studied beforehand by the Snowy Mountains Hydro-Electric Authority, according to Professor L.D. Pryor in his 1982 report for IUCN.

Rainstorms which before the fire produced peak flows of 60-80 cubic metres (2,120-2,825 cu ft), after the fire produced peaks of 370 cubic metres (13,065 cu ft) — four times more runoff. The load of suspended sediment (mostly soil) at a flow rate of 60-80 cubic metres was increased 100 times, according to Pryor. One rainstorm seven months after the fire caused record sediment concentrations in Wallace's Creek: the river water contained 14.4% sediment, by weight, equivalent to 115,000 tonnes per day.

The hydro-electric authority estimated from the increased flow and the increased sediment concentration that the total sediment load in Wallace's Creek was probably 1,000 times greater than before the fire.

One does not need to destroy forests to produce such results. In 1959, a rangefire consumed shrubs and other vegetation in carefully studied dry scrub rangeland of Arizona. In the months after the fire, water runoff increased sixfold and sediment load increased 270-fold, according to Pryor.

Pryor found that reforestation and other soil conservation measures could decrease floods. The small, 36-hectare (88-acre) watershed of Pine Tree Branch (a "branch" is a small river) in Tennessee (US) had not only been denuded of pine trees but had become so eroded that agriculture was abandoned on it in the mid-1940s. In the early 1950s, furrows were made along contour lines, diversion ditches were dug and gulleys were blocked. The watershed was replanted in pines. By the mid-1950s, the creek's water yield had been halved, which meant that the watershed itself was getting much of the other half. Peak flows had been reduced by 90% and sediment yield by 96%.

"Thus a flash-flood regime with very high sediment transport has been replaced by a steady flow of half the quantity of clean water", writes Pryor.

The "sponge effect" of trees, grass and crops — whereby the land absorbs rainfall and then releases it slowly over a long period of time — has also been studied by Professor Anders Rapp of Lund University (Sweden). His monitoring of surface runoff on gently sloping soil in Tanzania found that no erosion occurred and almost all rainwater was retained under a natural cover of grass and bush with widely scattered trees where no grazing took place. On land with millet cultivation, 25% of the rainwater ran off, bringing with it 78 tonnes of topsoil per hectare per year (32 tonnes/acre/year). Completely uncovered land — after harvest and grazing or burning of straw — lost 50% of the rainwater and 146 tonnes of topsoil per hectare per year (59 tonnes/acre/year). The connection between floods and deforestation is confirmed by historical examples cited by Ward. Floods on the Arno River in north-central Italy led Gianbattista Vico del Cilento in 1334 to recommend a government-sponsored reforestation programme. The work was never done, and Florence continues to suffer major floods, like the 1966 disaster which severely damaged the art galleries.

In 1797, a French engineer concluded that lowland flooding by Alpine rivers was a direct result of deforestation in the mountains. In 1890, the French government began reforesting the Hautes-Alpes, and it was reported that as the work continued, floods became fewer and smaller.

Early North American colonists noted a relationship between forest clearance, especially by burning, and flooding; and they pushed for reforestation programmes.

The introduction of Western agricultural practices into Southeast Asia, especially clear weeding between rows of long-standing crops such as rubber, caused flooding and erosion. When planters began turning their rubber plantations into man-made forests, with vegetation between trees, the problems eased.

Ward's review concentrated on temperate areas. In the tropics, the relationship between deforested watershed and fiercer floods is much stronger, due to the nature of the rainfall, types of soil and even types of vegetation in the tropics. Rain in the humid tropics tends to concentrate over a few months; over 70% of India's annual rainfall comes during 100 days of the Southwest Monsoon. In the drier tropics it tends to concentrate in a few hard storms in a few months. The soil must cope with much more rainwater during rains than in the temperate zones.

The tropical rainforests offer the best examples of how trees can limit the flow of rainwater into major rivers, and how felling these forests can exacerbate flooding. The forest canopy absorbs the rain's impact, physically protecting the soil from erosion. On the forest floor, "the leaf litter in varying stages of decay, the humus-rich topsoil and the spread of roots and former root passages, especially in the topsoil layers, acts indirectly as a sponge and filter to the heavy and often precipitous rainfall of the tropics. This is especially the case in monsoonal areas and at the beginning of the monsoon", wrote British forester John Wyatt-Smith in 1984. "The sponge effect reduces flash flooding and erosion... It is not often sufficiently realised that the natural vegetative cover is the best protective cover that can be provided in most circumstances and moreover that it is by far the cheapest method", he added.

The soil under most tropical moist forests is sandy or lateritic. When trees are cleared for agriculture, logging or to make roads, these soils tend to either erode or bake brick-hard. Forest does not return, and as there is little organic matter in the soil, grasses and crops do poorly.

In 1983, the border area of southern Brazil and northeastern Argentina was struck by severe floods. Some Argentinians blamed the floods on deforestation in Brazil. In Brazil's Parana state adjacent to the area, forests have diminished from 85% coverage in 1930 to 8% in 1980.

World Bank environmentalist Robert Goodland notes that intact forests provide such services as flood control; groundwater recharge; protection of river navigation; maintenance and restoration of soil fertility; control of landslides and erosion; prevention of sedimentation in rivers, reservoirs and irrigation systems; suppression of large fluctuations of plant and animal populations; buffering of the climate; and purification of air and water by acting as a sink for carbon dioxide and various pollutants.

"Substitution of even tiny components of this environmental protection service — such as by flood and erosion control methods applied to deforested lands and relief supplies for flood-ravaged communities — consumes inordinate quantities of resources and human energy that would be better applied elsewhere. This waste is entirely avoidable at low cost by leaving adequate protective forests intact", according to Goodland.

Even in the drier tropics vegetation can still shield the soil from heavy rainfall, slow down runoff and return water to the atmosphere. The impermeability of most cleared tropical soils can cause especially dangerous floods when hillsides are deforested.

The Himalayas

The Himalayas are a vast water machine; through snow melt and their blocking of moisture-laden winds, they send water southwards in the three great rivers of the Indian subcontinent: the Indus, the Ganges and the Brahmaputra. The mountains water a vast stretch of northern India, and much of Pakistan, Burma and Bangladesh.

Growing populations are stripping the forests from the habitable areas on the southern slopes of these mountains. And floods are increasing throughout the Himalayan watershed. Annual flood losses in India are today 14 times what they were in the 1950s.

"Most floods (in India) are the direct result of deforestation", flatly proclaims A.K. Dey, in the Indian journal *Disaster Management.*

British forester John Wyatt-Smith reported in 1984: "The heavy deforestation of the Himalayas during the past 30 years has led to increasing erosion and flooding during the monsoon months. One source estimates that in 1978 the direct damage to property caused by the monsoon totalled more than $2 billion, and the dry season water flows of the Ganges basin have declined by 18% over 1973-78."

During those 1978 floods, some of the worst in India's history, 2,000 people drowned, 66,000 villages were inundated and 40,000 cattle died.

"Many Indian officials are beginning to wonder whether their chronic flood problems can be ameliorated without a restoration of forest cover in the increasingly denuded hills of northern India and Nepal", writes Erik Eckholm. "According to India's National Commission on Floods, the area annually afflicted by floods now averages 40 million hectares (100 million acres), compared to 25 million hectares (62 million acres) three decades ago. The populations of flood-prone areas are increasing rapidly. Indian expenditures to offset flood damages averaged $250 million a year between 1953 and 1978", Eckholm added.

"The rate of depletion of forests in the Himalayan ranges, which represent a quarter of India's forest reserves, is so great that this mighty mountain chain could become barren by the first half of the next century", according to *The State of India's Environment: 1982,* a report by non-governmental organisations. "From Kashmir (far west) to Assam (far east) the story is the same. Below 2,000 metres (6,500 feet) there are literally no forests left. In the middle Himalayan belt, which rises to an average height of 3,000 metres (9,800 feet), the forest area, originally estimated at being a third of the total area, has reduced to a mere 6-8%", it said.

The report documents the increasing floods, erosion and deaths to people and cattle from the landslides which erosion can bring. It charges that India's flood control programme has failed in that "the area affected (by floods) and the economic damage has increased sharply over the last 30 years". Only 17 of India's 1,554 large dams were built for flood control purposes; many of those built to irrigate and store water are rapidly silting up due to soil erosion, also a result of deforestation.

In 1978, the Indian government estimated that one in every 20 people in the nation was vulnerable to flooding. Between June and September of that year, 46,000 villages were flooded, over 8.75 million hectares (21.6 million acres) were inundated and crops from 3.5 million hectares (8.6 million acres) were lost. Damage was estimated at some $60 million.

In 1980, heavy monsoon rains again inundated much of the northern plain, and killed 1,800 people. Many of these died in collapsing houses, which have little resistance to floods. In Uttar Pradesh, holes appeared in dykes due to poor materials and construction methods.

Massive erosion of topsoil across a large farming area is itself a disaster, but the sort of disaster to which relief agencies tend not to respond. However, erosion also adds to flood danger as deposited silt raises river beds, making less room for water. If embankments are built to keep the river on its course, then these expensive works must be constantly raised as erosion puts more soil onto the river bottom. An OXFAM report on disasters in West Bengal found that along the Ganges "the predominant flood problem is in the areas on the northern bank of the river. The damage is caused by the innumerable northern tributaries spilling over the banks and changing their courses. The extent of the damage shows a pattern of increase from west to east (downstream along the Ganges) and from south to north (toward the hills). In West Bengal the problem appears to be due to the congestion of damaged channels and unauthorised encroachments on the floodplain." The OXFAM report adds:

> "Floods are now an annual feature, and there are many flash floods. The problem in the main is due to the reduced and inadequate capacity of the river channels due to silting caused by the devastation of forests in the catchment areas which leads to heavy soil erosion and heavy runoff. The increased utilisation of floodplains for agriculture and urbanisation and the unplanned development of valuable areas liable to floods has increased the amount of damage over the years. There is every indication that it will continue to increase."

The Embankment and Drainage Department reports that the high water mark at Dibrugarh on the Brahmaputra River in northeast Assam — before that river has had time to attain much size — has risen gradually over the past 40 years, and since 1960 it has always been above the "danger mark".

Much of the cause of deforestation in Assam is immigration from Bangladesh. The combination of rising populations and steadily rising waters will bring more disasters. State governments are largely responsible for flood control measures in India, yet as the catchment areas lie outside Assam, the state can do little. And there is little cooperation between the departments of flood control, soil conservation and forests, as each looks to its own problems.

China

China has proven ability to organise its population of over one billion people to undertake massive public works. But the people's efforts have had only limited success against floods.

In the Yangtze in the south and the Yellow River (Huang Ho) in the north, China is coping with two of the world's most intractable streams of water. An 1871 flood on the Yangtze pushed the water 85 metres (275 feet) above its normal level in the gorges downstream from Chongqing, and a river steamer caught on a rock was left 35 metres (120 feet) above the river when the waters subsided. A 1954 flood caused the evacuation of 10 million people in the lower valleys, according to reports in China.

The Yellow River — also known as "China's Shame" — has killed more people than any other single feature of the Earth's surface, according to British geologist Tony Waltham. People have been channelling it, draining it and building levees (dykes along the river bank) since the first major works in 2356 BC. In 1887, the Yellow River flooded, killing between 900,000 and two million people by drowning and starvation due to loss of crops; and in 1931 one of the world's worst floods left 1-3.7 million people dead. In 1938 the levees were breached on purpose to stop the invading Japanese army. This held back the invasion, but killed 500,000 of the local population.

The Yellow River flows 4,000 km (2,500 miles) through northern China's yellow loess soils, picking up so much silt that by the time it reaches Kaifeng — with another 800 km (500 miles) to go to the sea across the Yellow Plain — it may be 40% silt. The silt is continuously being deposited in the river bed, so the river bed is continuously rising. Thus the dykes along the side of the river are being built even higher. So for much of its way across the Yellow Plain the river is eight metres (25 feet) above the surrounding fields. Major floods have changed the course of the river so much that the mouth has moved 435 km (270 miles).

Both rivers have vast watersheds which deliver rainwater quickly to the river, and rapid deforestation has worsened flooding problems faster than earthworks could alleviate them. In 1981 Sichuan province was hit by the worst flooding in decades, affecting 10 million people in 135 of the province's 212 counties. Wang Yun, a journalist for the agency China Features, interviewed Chinese experts for Earthscan; these blamed the floods on deforestation along the upper reaches of the Yangtze.

Deforestation of this once heavily wooded province began early last century when trees were cut to build imperial palaces. The 1958 steel-making campaign during Mao's "Great Leap Forward", using timber to fuel small back-yard iron smelting furnaces, led to further indiscriminate felling; later, forests were destroyed to create farmland for the 1960s "grain first" campaign. Vegetation cover, down to 19% in 1949, dropped to 13.3% recently. Half the agricultural counties in central Sichuan have below 3% tree cover, and some below 1%.

There are similar deforestation problems along the more accessible parts of the Yellow River. Even on subtropical Hainan Island in the South China Sea, vegetation cover has dropped from 25% to 7% over the past three decades.

The Chinese are convinced that reforestation can help prevent flood

League of Red Cross Societies

A family waits out a flood in the Bahia Negra region of Paraguay. Much of South America on both sides of the Andes range is becoming more prone to flooding as the highlands are deforested.

disasters. In 1981, the Sichuan Forestry Research Institute found that in the upper Jialing tributary of the Yangtze, where vegetation covered 15.7% of the watershed, a rain of 241.8 mm (9.5 inches) caused a flow 42.6% of flood volume. In another section, where the vegetative cover was only 3.5%, rains of 111.4 mm (4.5 in) caused a flow 68.1% of flood volume.

The government has set ambitious reforestation goals. Sichuan is meant to double its present forest cover by the end of the century.

But recent reports from China indicate that though the people can be persuaded to plant trees, they do not always find it in their interests to keep the trees growing. Canadian environmentalist Vaclav Smil quotes a Ministry of Forestry paper which says that of the huge numbers of trees planted since 1949, no more than a third have survived. He also quotes a Chinese folk saying: "Trees everywhere in spring, just half left by summer, no care taken in autumn, all trees gone by winter."

The Chinese have been experimenting with using vegetation as actual flood barriers. Wang reported that one village along the Jialing suffered little damage in the 1981 floods because it had planted along the river a 1,500-metre-long (5,000-foot) belt of bamao, a reed with long sturdy roots, interspersed with trees. A nearby village which had not taken such precautions lost its soil and had its land reduced to stone slabs.

The Andes

The Andes, like the Himalayas, are rapidly losing their topsoil as people living on their slopes try to get too much from this fragile environment. In 1983, floods and landslides along the coast of Ecuador killed scores and left $400 million worth of crop and property damage; Bolivia suffered record floods in its agriculturally-rich eastern lowlands; and in Peru, rains pelted the normally dry western slopes of the Andes, washing away whole villages and sweeping buses off mountain highways near the capital, Lima. The Peruvian government declared four northern provinces to be in states of emergency, and epidemics of typhoid and dysentery broke out among the victims.

These rains — and much of the rest of the world's peculiar weather in 1983 — were blamed on "El Niño" (The Christchild), the warm, southern-flowing current which begins running against the northern-flowing, colder Humboldt current off the west coast of Latin America at about Christmas of each year. In nine years out of 10, it subsides quickly and lets the Humboldt re-assert itself. In 1983 it did not stop in northern Peru; it instead moved far down the coast of Chile.

Its exact mechanics and its effects across the Pacific and on the high atmospheric "jetstreams" are in doubt, but the magnitude of its effects upon the weather are not. Locally it replaces cold, dry air with warm, wet air, and warm water piles up against western Latin America. This can cause rainfalls 10 times higher than usual in the Andean nations. But El Niño's movement also appears to shift the southern high altitude jetstream southwards, and this in turn moves the northern hemisphere jetstream southwards.

In 1983, El Niño was associated with floods and storms in western Latin America, the US Gulf of Mexico coast and Cuba, the western United States and Polynesia; and with droughts in Australia, Indonesia, the Philippines, India, Sri Lanka and southern Africa. (It was not blamed for the US drought.)

El Niño has overreached itself before. The 1965 extreme El Niño decimated the anchoveta fish upon which Peru's fishmeal industry was based. Extreme manifestations of El Niño will no doubt occur again, and each time another extreme El Niño comes along, the Andean states are more prone to floods due to overcultivation, urbanisation and deforestation.

Peasants are particularly poor throughout the Andean region. In 1976, the per capita Gross Domestic Product (GDP) of the five Andean countries (Bolivia, Colombia, Ecuador, Peru and Venezuela) averaged $960; but the agricultural GDP per rural dweller was $445. Even in Venezuela, with a per capita GDP of $1,705, the agricultural GDP was only $422 per peasant. In Bolivia the agricultural GDP per "campesino" (rural peasant) was only $120.

In the mid-1970s the average Andean dweller was able to get only 75% of the protein he or she needed daily and 87.5% of the calories. As those were national averages, one can assume the rural poor did even worse. These countries must import growing amounts of wheat, barley, sorghum, maize, rice, oilseeds, oils, flour, fats and dairy products. As in the Sahel, the governments seem to focus more attention on importing food to feed their wealthier people than to strive for food self-sufficiency by improving the efficiency of the smallholder. The Andean region has the lowest area harvested per person of all the Latin American regions: 0.16 hectare per person (0.39 acre/person) as opposed to the Latin American average of 0.38 hectare per person (0.94 acre/person). And populations of countries such as Bolivia, Ecuador and Peru are all growing faster than the tropical Latin American average.

All of which puts tremendous human pressure on soils of the humid eastern slopes of the Andes, which get too much rain, and on those of the arid western slopes, which get too little.

All the Andean countries are suffering rapid erosion, which increases both proneness and vulnerability to drought and flood. A 1977 Colombian government report found that 75% of the land was affected by erosion in one way or another and that 31% had undergone massive displacement. Erosion affects at least 30% of the territory of Peru in its Andean region, both on the eastern and western slopes. As early as 1945, a study found that the rivers of Peru's narrow coastal strip were carrying off 632 million cubic metres (22.3 billion cubic feet) of sediment yearly, equivalent to the loss of topsoil from 316,000 hectares (781,000 acres) a year. The magnitude of Ecuador's erosion problem is similar to that in Peru, according to a 1982 report on Latin American resources by Peruvian forester Marc Dourojeanni. Most of the cultivated land of Venezuela's Andean region has been affected by moderate to severe erosion, according to Dourojeanni. Erosion is also reaching major proportions in Venezuela's lowlands "because of the lack of cohesion of soils, the high degree of erosion caused by the prevailing rainfall, the low infiltration rate of the soil, and exposure of the soil to rainfall because of the intensive agriculture carried out there".

Dourojeanni could find few data on erosion in the Amazon region, but concluded that "a better idea of the extent of erosion in the Amazon basin is given by the increase in the frequency of flooding in the low areas, and by the growing extent of this phenomenon as well as the ever greater constraints being placed on river navigation". Yet these floods are controlled by what happens on the eastern slopes of the Andes (especially in Ecuador and Peru), "where extensive and chaotic migratory agriculture is practised".

A 1980 study found that over a 10-year period there was a neat correlation between the Amazon River's flood peaks at Iquitos, Peru, and deforestation rates in the high and medium parts of the river's Peruvian watershed.

Accelerating deforestation in the Andes will ensure that flooding will become more serious. Ecuador has 18.2 million hectares (45 million acres) of "woody vegetation". Over 1976-80, it lost 300,000 hectares (740,000 acres) of forest per year — 240,000 hectares (590,000 acres) of this listed as "productive forest", according to a 1981 FAO/UNEP study of tropical forests. This rate was expected to increase to 340,000 hectares (840,000 acres) lost per year over 1981-85. All the Andean countries except Venezuela expected increasing rates of deforestation.

Floods and droughts

Overuse of land, deforestation and the resulting erosion can make tropical land more prone to both floods and droughts. The two apparently opposing disasters are intimately connected.

British geographer Roy Ward writes of Bangladesh: "It is ironical that in an area through which flows the discharge from the second largest river system in the world, flood is followed by drought because the floods, which assume such vast proportions, often inundating one-third of the total land area of Bangladesh, are not adequately controlled. Destruction by flood is thus followed by drought-provoked famine in a vicious and, as yet, unending circle."

Robert Goodland of the World Bank, writing about the Sahel, sketches in the other half of this vicious circle: "Livestock production exceeding the carrying capacity of an area leads to the widespread — and increasing — syndrome of overgrazing, involving deterioration of grazing land, particularly around watering holes; loss of annual and then perennial vegetation; compaction of soils; and subsequent increases in erosion and flooding." Thus the overgrazing, deforestation and overcultivation associated with drought also leads to loss of topsoil and compaction of the soil; this means that water is carried over the ground quickly, allowing little absorption by the soil. The rush of water may or may not be seen as a "flood", but if the water runs off the ground without sinking in, crops react as if in a drought, like the "pseudo-droughts" of Haiti described at the beginning of the previous chapter.

On the Indian subcontinent, the areas with more marginal rainfall — Baluchistan, Sind, Uttar Pradesh — are most prone to both drought and flood years.

Thus in arid and semi-arid lands, measures to make drought-prone land more productive are very similar to flood-control methods. Trees are planted. Gulleys are blocked. Dry riverbeds are channelled so that agricultural land gets the water. Any dam or barrage or even line of shrubs which slows down the movement of water, encouraging it to sink into the soil, is a reasonable measure against "drought". (See "Drought" section of final chapter.)

Gunnar Hagman, in the 1984 Swedish Red Cross report *Prevention Better*

Tom Learmonth/Earthscan

Floods in Dhaka, Bangladesh. Some 15% of the nation's 90 million people live less than three metres (10 feet) above sea level. The wealthy tend to live higher — and drier.

than Cure provided a list of the types of areas in which human action makes soils vulnerable for various reasons, and makes the land prone to either flood or drought, or in many cases both:

* Areas where the population density and/or the population growth is highest and resource needs are most intense: China, India, Bangladesh, Middle East, sub-Saharan Africa, Central America.
* Areas of exceptional demand for fodder, owing to high livestock density: Iraq, Ethiopia, Central America, Uruguay.
* Areas in which vegetation is particularly sensitive and at the same time attractive for exploitation: tropical rainforests of Brazil, Zaire and Indonesia.
* Areas where there are acute fuelwood shortages: Nepal, India, Ethiopia, the Sahel, Bolivia.
* Arid and semi-arid areas where rainfall is limited and erratic: parts of India, the Middle East, the Sudano-Sahelian region, parts of Chile and Brazil.
* Mountain slopes and river basins where the soil easily runs off: India, Nepal, Ethiopia, Central America, Colombia, Peru and Bolivia.

Vulnerable urban poor

In the North, physical barriers and other flood-control mechanisms, along with well-enforced zoning laws and building codes, decrease the population's vulnerability to floods.

Yet in the major cities of the South, between 30% and 75% of urban populations live completely outside the law. They build their own houses; they squat on privately-owned or government land; or they pay a fee to occupy illegally-subdivided land. In most major Third World cities, the proportion of the urban population living in such illegal settlements is increasing. Obviously, the wealthy do not want dangerous land: land prone to flooding by rainfall, tides or storm surges, or hills and ravines prone to landslides during rainstorms or earthquakes. So this land is available to the poor.

In Guayaquil, Ecuador, it was estimated in 1975 that 60% of the population of over a million lived in squatter communities built over tidal swampland. These settlements consist of small, bamboo and timber houses standing on poles above mud and polluted water. For some people, dry land is a 40-minute walk over a network of timber catwalks. The whole community is prone to flooding and storm surges.

In 1983, when El Niño brought floods to the huge Guayaquil shantytown known as Guasmo, rising water coated with a green slime brought the contents of the toilet pits into the houses, and "patches of rash laced the residents' skin", according to Thomas Canby of *National Geographic* (US) magazine. Typhoid struck many of the shantytown dwellers.

Guayaquil is a port set within steep mountains. As the poor spread across the mudflats, the rest of the city spreads up the steep slopes, and the government has done little to control development. (Laws forbid construction above 3,000 metres (9,840 feet), but the Church and the army, two powerful forces in Ecuador, were the first to ignore these laws.) Land clearing for building has meant increasing landslides after heavy rains, and again it is the poorer people who live in the path of such slides. During the 1983 flooding hundreds of houses slid down Guayaquil's steep slopes.

Other Latin American and Caribbean cities face similar threats. Shantytown dwellers on the steep slopes of Rio de Janeiro (described by one European geographer as "of Alpine difficulty") are not killed and injured by floods themselves. Instead, they and their houses slide down the slopes when rainstorms loosen the soil. In Recife, Brazil, many of the poor live on the frequently flooded tidal flats, subsisting on the crabs with which they share this ground. "La Perla" (The Pearl), a major slum of San Juan, Puerto Rico, is often inundated at high tide.

In Mexico City, some 1.5 million people live on the drained lake bed of Texcoco, land which either floods or becomes a bog when it rains (in the dry season it is subject to dust storms). Port-au-Prince, the capital of Haiti, is another port surrounded by steep hills. These hills, like much of the rest

Bangladeshi boys besides their flooded hut. Natural disasters strike hardest at society's vulnerable: the young, the old, the malnourished.

---

of the country, have been so deforested and eroded that there is nothing to stop the water after a tropical storm, and flash floods kill people in the city streets.

Many of Asia's poorest squatters live on floodplains. Much of the expansion of Delhi has been onto the floodplain of the Yamuna River. Many of the city's 600,000 squatters, plus 700,000 people living in unauthorised subdivisions and 150,000-200,000 people living essentially in campsites, are vulnerable to flooding — as are wealthier people who occupy their land legally. In 1980, the Yamuna flooded, forming a lake of some 130 sq km (50 sq miles).

Of Bangkok's population of about five million, at least 1.2 million live in slums and illegal settlements. Many of these settlements are on swampy ground prone to flooding, and the floods following Typhoon Georgia in October 1983 made many such people homeless. Other Asian cities with flood-prone shantytowns include Calcutta, Dhaka (Bangladesh), Manila (Philippines), and Port Moresby (Papua New Guinea).

African capitals in which large numbers of the poorer people are in danger of inundation include Monrovia (Liberia) and Lagos.

68

This flood in the northern Haitian village of Limbé was caused as much by poor drains as by rainfall and deforestation.

Floodplains

Humans have long been attracted to floodplains. Here rivers deposit the topsoil picked up elsewhere, so the land is fertile. Floodplains are both flat and near water, so irrigation, ploughing and transport (usually aided by the river) are all made easier. The heavy settlement along the lower reaches of Egypt's Nile, India's Ganges, Bangladesh's Brahmaputra-Padma, the United States' Mississippi, the Yellow River and Yangtze of China, and the Tigris and Euphrates of what is now Iraq are all examples of floodplain civilisations.

But rivers do not go on laying down ever greater amounts of sedimentation in a floodplain. The inflow of sediment equals the net outflow over a long period of time. "Seen in this light, floods are simply part of the complete range of hydro-geomorphological events operating within the drainage basin", according to British geographer Roy Ward. In other words, floods are normal in floodplains. Yet floodplains remain desirable places to live, not only in agricultural societies, but also in industrial countries where the floodplains often host large capitals which use the river water for industry and its mouth as a harbour for shipping. Washington DC, Paris and London were built on terraces overlooking rivers. But these and other cities built above rivers have since spread out onto the floodplains.

China's Yellow River — because of constant silting and the constant raising of levees — runs above its floodplain. Each year an average of 8,300 sq km (3,200 sq miles) is flooded. The water cannot recede into the river because the river is above it. There are no hills on the plain and no escape routes for the residents, whose only hope is to keep building the levees higher.

The Brahmaputra-Ganges delta, which occupies most of the country of Bangladesh, is almost as dangerous, but has been subjected to fewer human works. Here the hazards are both floods coming downriver and the rains and storm surges from the sea accompanying cyclones. In 1970, the rivers were up, there were high tides and a cyclone pushing water onshore. This combination spread water over 10,400 sq km (4,000 sq miles) and killed some 150,000-300,000 people (estimates vary).

"In the coastal plains of the United States, when storms and flooding threatens, upwards of a million people are now routinely evacuated", said US geographer Robert Kates at the World Climate Conference in 1979. "Yet in Bangladesh, where perhaps 15% of the country's 90 million inhabitants live less than 10 feet (3 metres) above sea level, 150,000 died when the sea surged inland during the tropical cyclone of 1970."

Disaster experts have long been amazed by the way the poor moved back into low-lying areas around the Bay of Bengal only a few weeks after wind and water have killed relatives and wrecked their homes. Population pressure is pushing more and more people out onto the "chars" (a series of shifting islands) around the delta. These are extremely fertile, and people extend cultivation areas by building dams between the islands and farming part of the reclaimed riverbed. Yet these islands are so vulnerable to the floods and storm surges following cyclones that the raised house platforms, tied-down roofs and tree shelterbelts that offer some protection slightly further inland are of little help here. There is little money for more elaborate protective devices, as the farmers are often paying one-third of their crops to absentee landlords — who do not share the danger.

Yet most are making a carefully considered choice. According to Ward, residents of the coastal lowlands of Bangladesh are well aware of the hazards, "but do not migrate even when they know of opportunities elsewhere. The strong incentives to remain include the prospect of acquiring more land through government-sponsored flood embankment schemes, family ties and the existence of relief and rehabilitation programmes." Here, it is not only fertile land, but the very existence of outside support which is a factor in keeping people in dangerous areas.

Chapter 4

Tropical cyclones and other winds

"You don't need a weatherman
To know which way the wind blows."
US folk singer Bob Dylan

Humans can make their environment more prone to floods and droughts. They can even increase the likelihood of earthquakes by lubricating the earth's underground rock strata. But they have found no way of bringing cyclones upon themselves. Cyclones just happen.

A tropical cyclone is an intense tropical storm with windspeeds of over 118 kilometres per hour (73 mph) — Force 12 on the Beaufort Scale of Wind Force. Cyclones usually tear away anemometers (wind gauges), so their speeds are rarely measured accurately. But most are thought capable of sustained speeds of 200 kph (125 mph) over large areas, with gusts up to 400 kph (250 mph).

Such tropical windstorms are called hurricanes in the Caribbean, Atlantic and North American regions; cyclones in the Indian Ocean; typhoons in the Pacific; and baguio around the Philippines. All of these are the same phenomenon. About 80-100 tropical cyclones develop each year from low-pressure areas in tropical oceans, usually between latitudes 5 and 30 degrees on either side of the equator, but more usually in the north. The biggest storms are found in the west Pacific.

A cyclone begins to form when moist air heated by the sun rises from the surface of the warm tropical seas and is funnelled upwards in a natural updraft. As this moist air rises, it cools and condenses into rain. This condensation feeds back into the air large amounts of heat, which add to the force of the storm's updraft and which stokes the power of the cyclone. Air continues to go spiralling up, and hot moist air rushes in from all sides to replace it and to feed the updraft. The winds spiral around an "eye", an area of calm and light rains a few kilometres across. The cyclone itself may be between 100 and 200 km (60-125 miles) in diameter with a vertical depth of 11-19 km (7-12 miles). But the diameter of the greater storm may be 200-500 km (125-310 miles). Winds are accompanied by torrential rains and can push ocean water high onto beaches (the "storm surges" that often accompany cyclones). Cyclones move forward at some 16-32 kph (10-20 mph)

Sophie Baker/Earthscan

The aftermath of a Philippines typhoon which killed 500. In the Philippines, a middle-income nation, the average disaster kills 220 people. In Ethiopia, among the world's poorest nations, the average disaster kills 6,440.

Sophie Baker/Earthscan

over tropical seas and sometimes at up to 80 kph (50 mph) in the higher latitudes before blowing out.

Storms tend to have their beginnings a great distance from where they achieve cyclone status. Hurricanes which affect the Caribbean and North America often begin on the other side of the Atlantic as far east as the Cape Verde Islands off the coast of Africa. Here, just north of the equator, the southeast trade winds of the southern hemisphere meet the northeast trade winds of the northern hemisphere at the Inter-Tropical Convergence Zone (ITZ) — the area sailors call the "Doldrums" — because there is little wind. As these trade winds collide, the earth's rotation causes the air to move in an anti-clockwise direction. In the southern hemisphere, this movement is clockwise.

Despite intense research, it is not known why some storms become hurricanes. Most do not. Others, given the right conditions, travel the width of the Atlantic, reach the appropriate size and windspeed, are given the title hurricane and named. Once a tropical cyclone moves over land it quickly begins to lose force.

Warning, prevention and buildings

No two tropical cyclones take the same route, and their erratic nature makes warning both more difficult and more necessary. In the West Indies, routine monitoring of the tropical low pressure areas which may precede hurricanes has increased the probability of early warning to almost 100%. Most forecasts can give 24 hours warning of the expected arrival time and the force of the storm.

Elsewhere, forecasting and tracking has also improved. But Third World governments have had less success in getting the information to exposed populations. Peasants in Bangladesh, the Philippines and Central America either do not receive the warnings or have no way of evacuating the area, or both. When Hurricane Lisa hit the area around La Paz, Mexico, in 1976, it killed over 500 people. Most of the casualties and the worst damage was in the shantytown of Chimitla, a community of 10,000 people outside La Paz. The city mayor's office said later that the residents of Chimitla had not received or heeded warnings to leave. Several shanties were carried up to 10 km (6 miles) by the floodwaters.

But warning has been more successful than prevention. A US experiment ("Operation Stormfury") which began in 1960 has routinely sent planes into the eyes of hurricanes to study them and to "seed" the clouds with silver iodide crystals to speed precipitation. Results have been inconclusive, but the experimenters claim to have reduced maximum wind speeds by 10-15%. The US government has been hesitant to try large-scale experiments for fear of lawsuits from thousands of residents of the US Gulf of Mexico coastline if a seeded storm hit land and damaged property. An idea to dissipate the force of hurricanes by exploding nuclear bombs in their eyes remains (perhaps fortunately) at the idea stage.

Cyclones cause an average of 10% loss among buildings, according to the Munich Reinsurance Company. But lesser windstorms can also cause a great deal of damage. Gales (Beaufort Force 8: 63-74 kph, or 39-46 mph) cause 1% loss among buildings, but as such storms occur 10 times as often as cyclones, they do roughly the same amount of damage to structures.

Obviously, sturdier, better designed buildings can better withstand wind. This improvement is happening naturally in the Caribbean, as over the years people have switched from wooden to masonry houses, the latter standing up better to hurricanes. (But masonry is more vulnerable than wood to earthquakes, another Caribbean hazard.) Few buildings are "blown over" in a cyclone; most explode due to low pressure on their outsides. The wind carries off the pieces. Thus light, open buildings may better resist cyclones than tightly closed concrete structures. And leaving windows and doors open is a standard precaution.

Six cyclones struck French Polynesia within five months in 1983, killing 17 people, leaving 25,000 homeless and destroying 10,000 houses. Many "modern" houses of brick and concrete were destroyed, but so were uncounted numbers of shacks of poorer families built of poles and corrugated iron. The houses which stood up best to the storms were the traditional island homes with thatched roofs. These have so many openings that the winds blow right through them. Marie-Therese and Bengt Danielsson, writing in the *Pacific Island Monthly* magazine, described how their 50-year-old traditional home — the oldest of its type on Tahiti — came through the cyclones unscathed.

Building against cyclones is cheaper than rebuilding. Nassau (Bahamas) has been largely rebuilt since a major hurricane destroyed it in 1929, but many of the modern office buildings and hotels were constructed without wind in mind, and were put dangerously close to the sea. It was estimated in the early 1970s that if a similar hurricane had struck the Bahamas then, over $50 million in damage would have been done, worth 11.6% of the Gross Domestic Product of the Bahamas. Yet the cost of precautions not taken — hurricane-proofing and keeping houses at least 25 metres (80 feet) back from the beachfront — would have added only 5% to building costs.

Storm surges

The greatest loss of life from cyclones is from drowning, by a ratio of about nine to one, according to the US Office of Emergency Preparedness. Most of these drownings are the result of "storm surges", in which coastal waters rise high above mean sea level. Cyclones have caused storm surges up to 7.5

74

Mark Edwards/Earthscan

Haiti: This was a mangrove forest — cleared by peasants for wood to make charcoal. Settlements inland are now vulnerable to hurricane storm surges.

---

metres (25 feet) high, sending floods several kilometres inland. Such surges are caused by a combination of factors, mainly winds pushing water ahead of them, and the "sucking" effect of the cyclone's action raising the sea level.

Along the US Gulf and Atlantic some six million people are exposed to storm surge damage. Australia, Bangladesh, China, India, Japan and Mexico also have long stretches of coast prone to these surges. In 1737, a storm surge killed up to 300,000 people in Calcutta and along the coast of what is now Bangladesh, and an 1876 storm surge killed another 215,000 people on that coast. The storm surge in 1970 in Bangladesh killed 150,000-300,000 people (see Chapter Three).

Agriculture is as vulnerable to cyclone damage as it is to the other climatological disasters. Many of the tropical countries most prone to cyclones rely on subsistence agriculture to feed their people and on agricultural commodities to earn the majority of their foreign exchange. The 1963 tropical storm Helena destroyed half the sugarcane crop and 95% of the banana crop on Guadeloupe. Hurricane Allen in 1979 destroyed 97% of St Lucia's banana plantations, 95% of St Vincent's, 75% of Dominica's and 40% of Grenada's, according to the London-based Latin America Bureau. But such statistics leave out damage in years following the disaster, which can be greater due either to general disruptions of plantations or to salt left in fields by storm surges. Hurricane Fifi hit Honduras in 1974, lowering banana production by 20% that year; in 1975, production was down 50%.

Tornadoes and inland winds

Strong winds can do great damage inland, but these are usually associated with local thunderstorms. In fact, the winds which perhaps do the most economic damage in the world have nothing to do with "disasters" at all, but are those steady winds which remove topsoil and moisture from cleared agricultural land in the tropics.

Tornadoes are the most severe inland windstorms, occurring all over the world — Europe, India, Japan, South Africa and Australia — but found mostly in the flat Midwestern United States. The US suffers about 1,000 tornadoes per year; and in 1974, 93 tornadoes struck the US Midwest in a period of two days, causing $1 billion in damage.

A tornado is "visible as a vortex, a whirlpool structure of winds rotating around a hollow cavity in which centrifugal forces produce a partial vacuum. As condensation occurs around the vortex, a pale cloud appears — the familiar and frightening tornado funnel. Air surrounding the funnel is also part of the tornado vortex; as the storm moves along the ground, this outer ring of rotating winds becomes dark with dust and debris, which may eventually darken the entire funnel" (a description published by the US Department of Commerce, 1966).

Tornadoes usually appear during warm, humid, unsettled weather and form several thousand metres above the earth's surface, often in conjunction with a thunderstorm. The tornado funnel is an extension of cumulo-nimbus storm clouds. Some funnels never touch the ground; others touch briefly before dissipating; but the destructive tornado travels with its base on the ground, bent by friction. Tornadoes normally average only 100 metres (110 yards) across and travel a few kilometres. But severe tornadoes can reach a width of over one kilometre (0.6 miles) and travel 300 km (185 miles). It has not been easy to measure tornado wind speeds, but these have often been estimated at upwards of 500 kph (310 mph). Such winds can destroy the toughest buildings. But tornadoes are such short-lived, unpredictable disasters that experts have generally taken the view that any "tornado- proofing" would simply not be cost-effective.

It is not clear why tornadoes form. Most scientists opt for a combination of two explanations: thermal (forces set up when a layer of cool air rests on top of warm air) and mechanical (slowly rotating air currents constrained by external forces, speeding ever faster as the radius of rotation decreases).

"Extratropical" storms occur in the area between the subtropical and polar climatic zones (35-70 degrees latitude). They are also known as winter storms, because they occur most frequently in the late autumn and winter when the

	Storm events 1960-1981	Number of people killed
Low-income economy		
Bangladesh	37	386,200
Burma	7	1,350
China	7	170
Haiti	6	5,800
India	26	24,930
Madagascar	9	970
Vietnam	6	7,480
Fr. Caribbean	5	100
Middle-income economy		
Hong Kong	7	510
Mauritius	7	15
Mexico	14	1,560
Philippines	39	5,650
South Korea	10	700
High-income economy		
Italy	5	110

Figure 10. Storm events (mainly tropical cyclones) 1960-81 (the USA is not included). The most serious disasters occurred in low-income Asian countries. (Source: Prevention Better than Cure, *Swedish Red Cross, 1984, based on League of Red Cross and USOFDA statistics, and World Bank indicators.)*

oceans are still warm but the polar air has become very cold. Such storms can be as wide as 1,500 km (930 miles) with maximum wind velocities of 200 kph (124 mph). They are a major hazard to shipping and have done severe damage across Europe. Wind velocities increase with increasing height above sea level, and buildings and hills can create jet affects which produce local damaging gusts.

Historically, storm tides associated with such events have caused great loss of life: 100,000 killed in the western Netherlands in 1421 and 8,000 killed in southern England in 1703 and the same number dead in Leningrad in 1824. But today there are more and better barriers against such tides.

The other main type of damaging windstorm is the monsoon storm, but these are only frequent and dangerous — from the point of view of winds — in the northwestern stretches of the Indian Ocean off the Horn of Africa in early summer, when the temperature contrasts between the Arabian Sea and the Indian subcontinent are greatest, according to the Munich Reinsurance Company.

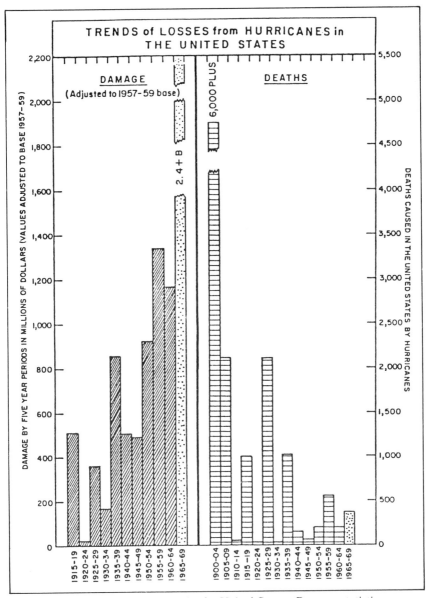

Figure 11. Losses from hurricanes in the United States. Damage statistics are based on 1957-59 construction costs. While damage has gone up, loss of life has decreased, due to better warning services and community preparedness. (Source: ESCAP, WMO and League of Red Cross Societies, 1977.)

78

WFP/FAO

Replacing seafront vegetation and mangrove forests with settlements makes residents vulnerable to cyclones and storm surges. Both combined to flatten this Philippines fishing village in 1977.

Vulnerability

Cyclones tend to affect island and coastal communities — the Caribbean, Philippines and Japanese islands. Here populations are often concentrated along coasts, either as fishing/farming communities or port cities acting as centres of trade and commerce. River floodplains provide excellent farmland, but can become deathtraps during storm surges.

Altering the environment can make people and property more vulnerable to the effects of storm surges. Around the world, the "development" of tropical seafronts often means the destruction of coral reefs (to build marinas, causeways, airports or to open channels), mangrove and other seafront forests and the levelling of beach dunes. This activity clears paths which allow storm surges to reach humans and their property more quickly and forcefully.

The Philippines suffered 39 violent storms over 1960-81, with 5,650 killed. Bangladesh suffered 37 such disasters over the same period and lost 386,200 people. The Philippines coastline is many times longer than that of Bangladesh, yet it is reckoned that 20 million Bangladeshis are exposed to the effects of cyclones. Bangladesh has long since deforested most of its floodplains, and the rapid depositing of eroded soil from the Himalayas has made a smooth thoroughfare for floods moving down and storm surges moving up. The Philippines' varied coasts are more protected by reefs, mangroves and trees.

Also, the Philippines is a middle-income country, while Bangladesh is one of the world's poorest. The improved Filipino communications, warning services and community preparedness programmes save lives. A look at countries with five or more storm disasters between 1960 and 1981 confirms the link between low incomes and high death tolls (see Figure 10).

Storms cause the heaviest property losses in the developed countries. Experience in the US shows how increased development leads to higher property damage — as both the amount of property and its value grows — but to decreased deaths (see Figure 11). In 1915-19, US hurricane property damage was below $600 million; this rose erratically to over $2.4 billion for 1965-69 (dollars adjusted to 1957-59 base). In 1900-04, hurricanes killed more than 6,000 people; this toll fell fairly steadily to less than 500 deaths in 1965-69. The US government attributes the falling death toll to improved warning services and community preparedness programmes.

Cyclones are almost always accompanied by heavy rains — perhaps 250 mm (10 ins) in 12-48 hours, but often as high as 1,000 mm (40 ins) — which may add to the storm surge damage. As this rain strikes inland it may cause floods and mudslides. In such cases, the sort of human actions which increase vulnerability to floods also increase vulnerability to cyclones. Deforestation can increase flood vulnerability and proneness, but forests can also offer a bit of protection against wind damage. Studies from Cuba find that there is far less damage from wind in forested areas than in deforested zones.

Honduras, Hurricane Fifi and the poor

Around 1956, the US banana companies which had cleared and developed the fertile valleys off the major San Pedro Sula Valley in northern Honduras shifted from labour-intensive to capital-intensive production methods. The peasants could not farm the rich valleys, because they were either taken up by the banana plantations of the US companies United Brands and Standard Fruit, or by irrigated farms owned by the rich. (In Honduras, some 4% of the population owns 65% of the arable land.) So they moved up the valley sides, clearing the hillside forests to grow corn. This deforestation caused severe erosion; rivers flooded more frequently because they were silting up and because the rainwater was running into them more quickly from the watershed.

When Hurricane Fifi struck in 1974, its heavy rains turned the exposed soil of the hillsides into a liquid paste. Between 4,000 and 8,000 people were killed. One disaster expert claimed that the death toll was estimated by counts of human bodies passing certain river bridges over a given time. Post-Fifi aerial photographs showed hillsides which looked as if they had been raked with huge claws. The multinational companies and the wealthy farmers did not escape unscathed. Deforestation worsened river flooding, and losses in crop production and infrastructure in the valleys amounted to $350-450 million. The rich lost money and the poor lost their lives.

Later that same year Cyclone Tracy, with windspeeds similar to Hurricane Fifi (230-250 kph, 140-155 mph) struck the coastal city of Darwin on Australia's north coast. Forty-nine died in Darwin, 4,000-8,000 in Honduras. Both Darwin and northern Honduras are in major tropical cyclone areas and both had extensive warning facilities. But the warnings did not reach the Latin American hillside farmers. Darwin was almost completely evacuated before it was almost completely flattened.

Both places are *prone* to cyclones. But the social structure and underdevelopment of Honduras made the poor there *vulnerable* to cyclones. Darwin is prone but not vulnerable.

Chapter 5

Earthquakes

"The mountains skipped like lambs
and the hills like young sheep."
Description of earthquake,
The Bible, Psalm 114.

"God grant that the pillars of the earth may be
again fastened, and the equilibrium of both
natural and moral things restored."
Count Francesco Ippolito after the earthquake
in Calabria, Italy, of 1773.

Earthquakes have been written about for centuries, but only very recently have their mechanics become at least partially understood.

Before the theory of plate tectonics became widely accepted — only over the past two decades — suspected causes ranged from "deep volcanoes" to planet-girdling tunnels through which quakes travelled around the globe. Almost all theories saw them as "acts of God": a phrase which still appears today in insurance and other contracts. Thus, Europeans were neither surprised nor particularly bothered in the 17th and 18th centuries that God struck heathen lands. The disappearance beneath the sea of two-thirds of the Jamaican pirate and vice capital of Port Royal during a 1692 quake led to the jingle "Jamaica shou'd be shook! And lands like Sodom, all impure".

But Europe received a deep shock on 1 November 1755, when Lisbon, one of the richest cities of Christendom, was virtually wiped out by quake and fire, with an estimated 60,000 deaths. The Lisbon quake, according to British geologist Tony Waltham, was near "the maximum limit to the magnitude of earthquakes, dictated by the amount of strain that can accumulate in rocks at any depth before their failure". The event brought earthquakes to the attention of science, but little cause could be found besides the alleged wickedness of that city's inhabitants. (The event so shocked Europe that the King of France even vowed to give up his mistress.) Some historians feel that the Lisbon quake helped to contribute to the rejection by 18th century intellectuals of the idea of Divine Providence during the period known as the Enlightenment. Such destruction could not have been caused by a loving god.

It was not until 1929, when Alfred Wegener published his book, *The*

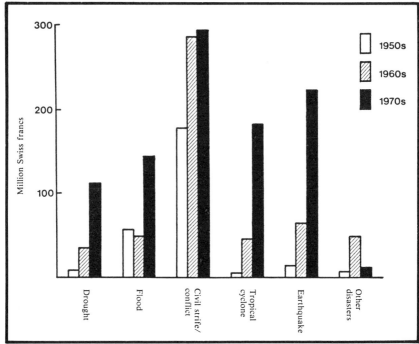

Figure 12. Donor response to the League of Red Cross Societies. These figures suggest that the most successful appeals are those for disasters with a heavy loss of life. However, this may be because the League issues more appeals for earthquake and war disasters. (Source: Prevention Better than Cure, *Swedish Red Cross, 1984.)*

Origins of Continents and Oceans, containing the theory of continental drift, that geologists had a reasonable explanation for quakes. According to the theory of plate tectonics, the earth's outer shell is divided into seven major and some smaller plates which are constantly pushing against, pulling away from or grinding past one another. The theory not only provides general explanations for earthquakes, volcanoes and some other geological phenomena, but also reassures humans that earthquakes are limited in area to plate boundaries. There are few within the plates, though there are occasional exceptions to this rule. (Not all geologists accept the theory of plate tectonics today.)

Earthquakes have an odd position in the field of disaster studies. They are the deadliest disaster. In the 1970s they killed 38,970 people per year, while cyclones came second with 34,360. (The average for that decade was extremely high due to the 242,000 people killed in the 1976 Tangshan, China, quake.) Earthquakes are also perhaps the most exciting, least understood, most poorly predicted of the major disasters. Thus they are given disproportionate attention, not only by journalists, but also by relief organisations and disaster experts.

Earthquakes are often taken as models when disasters are discussed at expert conferences, and influence responses to all other disasters, even to droughts, which require very different measures. (The current head of UNDRO's Disaster Prevention Branch is a seismologist.) Yet in terms of numbers of people affected per year during the 1970s, earthquakes (1.2 million) come at the bottom of the table, below drought (24.4 million), flood, civil strife/conflict and tropical cyclones (see Figure 12).

Where they happen

Some oceanic plates are pulling away from one another. Hot volcanic material emerges from the cracks to form mid-ocean ridges such as those in the Atlantic and the East Pacific. Elsewhere oceanic plates collide with and are forced under continental plates, pushing up mountain ranges, accompanied by earthquakes and volcanic eruptions. The oceanic Nazca plate of the southeast Pacific is pushing against the South American plate, forming the Andes range.

Collisions of continental plates can also force up mountain ranges and release compression energy in quakes. This is happening right across the northern Mediterranean (the Alps, and the earthquakes of northern Italy and Greece), through Iran and across northern India down through the Indonesian archipelago. India is a northern wedge of the Indo-Australian plate pushing northeastwards against the Eurasian plate to form the Himalayas.

Or two plates can slide along one another, the most famous example being the 965-km (600-mile) San Andreas Fault running from northern California to Mexico. This boundary between the Pacific and the American plates passes through San Francisco and Los Angeles, and most earthquake researchers believe this fault will be the scene of a major quake in the next few years.

Two-thirds of the world's large earthquakes have occurred in the "Ring of Fire" around the Pacific, (so called because of its active volcanoes). This ring stretches up the west coasts of South and North America into Alaska, across the Aleutians, down through Japan offshore of the continental landmass, through the Philippines, Indonesia and out through New Zealand. All quakes killing 100,000 or more people have occurred in Asia, most of these in China. A quake in Shensi province in 1556 killed 830,000 people, the biggest death toll ever in a single quake, according to the Munich Reinsurance Company.

The next most important zone stretches along the plate boundaries from Indonesia, along the Himalayas and the axis of the Mediterranean, according to Tony Waltham. Some 75% of the world's earthquake deaths in 1950-70 occurred in this zone, because it is more densely populated than the Circum-Pacific Belt.

In the western hemisphere, the most damaging earthquakes occur on the west coast of Central and South America. Quakes killing more than 10,000 have been recorded in Guatemala, Argentina, Chile, Colombia, Ecuador, Peru and Venezuela.

Another earthquake zone, bordering the Caribbean plate, is not very significant in terms of carnage, but has been studied recently in conjunction with treaties signed in 1983 to protect and develop the Caribbean region. Eight major quakes have killed about 16,000 people in the islands over the past 300 years. The Lesser Antilles experience between three and eight damage-causing quakes per century; but Port of Spain, Trinidad, gets 14 per century and Kingston, Jamaica, 17. Seismologists note that the Caribbean plate has been very quiet recently, and "it can therefore be concluded that the present deficits in earthquake energy release are temporary and will ultimately be compensated by higher than normal activity", according to a 1979 report by UNEP and the Economic Commission of Latin America. In other words, the Caribbean is due for more quakes.

The Caribbean has undergone rapid urbanisation over the past century. John Tomblin of UNDRO estimates that an earthquake hitting the Caribbean 100 years ago "might damage 5% of the total property and affect 5% of the Gross National Product. Today it might destroy 50% of all property and dislocate a similar proportion of industrial production for several years." (Similar figures could be derived for other rapidly developing areas in earthquake belts.) Many Caribbean cities — especially large hotels and apartment blocks — are now built on the waterfront on land reclaimed from the sea, which is unstable during earthquakes.

Earthquakes very rarely occur in Australia and most of Africa, though there have been major quakes in North Africa, including one in 1717 which killed 20,000 people in Algiers. Big earthquakes have also struck Egypt, Libya and Morocco.

Measuring the shocks

Dr Charles Richter of the California Institute of Technology drew up his "Richter scale" of earthquake magnitude in 1935; it is an open-ended scale measuring the vibrational energy of the shock. Theoretically, it has no upper limit, but it is thought that rocks would shatter before they could build up enough stored energy to release a quake of 10 on the scale. The Chilean earthquake of 1960 measured Richter 9.5. The scale is logarithmic, which means in effect that each single number higher on the scale indicates a release of 10 times as much energy as the previous figure. Two or slightly more quakes of Richter 8 occur each year. And for each step down the scale, there are roughly 10 times more quakes of that magnitude. Thus there are about 20 quakes yearly of magnitude seven and 200 of magnitude six.

In 1977, the scale was slightly revised and some of the magnitudes of historical quakes altered. The San Francisco quake of 1906, which killed 65 people, was demoted from 8.3 to 7.9; and the 1964 Alaska quake was promoted from 8.3 to 9.2. The major effect of this change was to produce confusion in the libraries of the world's newspapers and wire services.

But then journalists have always had problems with the Richter scale. The magnitude of a large quake anywhere in the world can be measured on a seismograph anywhere else in the world. So a seismological station in Sweden can announce a quake of a certain Richter magnitude in the Pacific long before anything is heard from the quake area. However, the intensity of the quake — the damage it does — depends not just on the magnitude but also on such factors as the distance from the quake epicentre to the damage area in question, soil and rock conditions, density of population and type of buildings. Richter magnitude can be a poor indication of damage. For instance, the 1976 Tangshan, China quake registered 7.6 on the Richter scale and killed 242,000 people (official Chinese figure; estimates outside China put the toll at up to 665,000). However, the 1964 Alaska earthquake midway between the cities of Anchorage and Valdez registered a much higher 9.2 but killed 100 people.

The Modified Mercalli scale is perhaps the best known of several scales for measuring earthquake intensity. It ranges from I (not felt except by a very few) to XII (damage total; waves seen on ground surfaces; lines of sight and level distorted; objects thrown upwards into the air). Mercalli scale measurements give a far better indication of the human impact than the Richter scale. But the former requires the judgement of experts at the scene, and by the time such a reading is available, journalists and the public have usually lost interest. Besides, there are several other conflicting intensity scales in use. So earthquakes continue to be judged by their Richter readings.

Mechanics and effects

Earthquakes usually last less than a minute, though the 1964 Alaska quake lasted more than three minutes. And there are records of quakes rumbling on for hours and even days.

Two of the three types of earthquake waves travel very fast through rocks. The primary "P" waves — compressional waves, as in sending a jolt through a line of connected rail cars — travel at about eight kilometres (5 miles) per second. The secondary "S" waves — sheer waves, as in sending waves through a rope by a quick up-down flick — move at about half this speed. It is this difference in speed which allows seismograph stations to pinpoint the epicentre of a quake. Yet the P and S waves are usually only measurable

El Asnam, Algeria, 1980. Some buildings collapsed; others were rocked off their foundations; but 80 per cent of all buildings were damaged.

on a seismograph. It is the surface waves, which move at about half the speed of the S waves, which do the earthquake damage.

After a major quake there may be a series of aftershocks — occasionally lasting many days — as the rocks "settle down" near the epicentre. Sometimes these can be measured only on instruments; sometimes they do little damage but keep a stricken population in a state of panic, and occasionally the aftershocks are major earthquakes in their own right. Of the 28 aftershocks in the 24 hours following the 1964 Alaska quake, 10 were "significantly large", according to British geologist Tony Waltham, who adds: "Aftershocks commonly make the clearing up operation after an earthquake both hazardous and ineffectual". Within the 20 days following the 1976 Guatemala earthquake, over 1,000 aftershocks were recorded.

The effects of earthquakes on buildings depend on the nature of the land upon which the building is sited, what the building is made of, its design, how well it is made and the nature of the earthquake shock. Bedrock, though it transports earth waves efficiently, is a much safer foundation than young, sedimentary soils. The latter can be turned into a virtual liquid during the shaking of a quake. In the 1964 Niigata, Japan, quake (7.5 Richter), the mud beneath one block of flats became so liquid that the building quietly settled onto its side, and unhurt occupants climbed from their windows and walked down the gently sloping outside walls. Yet in the 1967 Caracas, Venezuela quake (6.5), four high-rise buildings collapsed straight downwards, killing 200. All stood on alluvial soils which transmitted the vibrations to the buildings; as the wave frequency of the soil was the same as the natural frequency of the buildings, an undulating harmonic motion developed and the blocks shook to pieces.

Before 1971, there had been few cases when instruments were set up to actually measure surface waves during an earthquake. It was estimated that buildings were subjected to extra forces of about 5-10% the force of gravity during a moderate quake, and thus building codes were calculated on a force of 10%. Yet in the 1971 San Fernando, California quake, 200 strong motion recording seismographs — "accelerographs", for measuring the movement of buildings — recorded accelerations equal to the force of gravity. The maximum was 120%, according to Peter Verney, author of *The Earthquake Handbook*. The 1972 Managua quake recorded readings of 39% the force of gravity. Thus a great many of the world's "quake-proof" buildings are not.

Short, sharp, high-frequency shocks lasting a few seconds do not trouble modern, tall buildings; structures of two to four storeys are more vulnerable. But lower frequency vibrations lasting fractions of a minute can completely destroy tall buildings. Modern reinforced concrete buildings survive well. The concrete buildings which collapse are usually those in which the builder has taken shortcuts to save money, such as using poor concrete or too much sand.

There are basically two ways of building against earthquakes. The first is strength: reinforced concrete, steel frame, deep foundations and a light roof. The second is "weakness" which cannot be shaken apart. Traditional Japanese wood and paper houses held together well during earthquakes, as the shaking had no more effect on them than the shaking of a wicker basket. Wood almost always stands up to earthquakes better than masonry, but is in obvious danger of the fires which often break out after quakes. Photos of Charleston, South Carolina (US), after an 1886 quake show streets in which every apparently solid brick and masonry house is wrecked, and all the wood frame houses and shops appear untouched.

In the Caribbean, prone to both earthquakes and hurricanes, people have been gradually shifting from wood to masonry as the main building material. This change makes homes less vulnerable to hurricanes but more vulnerable to quakes.

Third World housing

Much Third World housing — such as tropical Asian one-storey structures of plant-matting walls and palm-frond roofs — are virtually earthquake-proof. But then few such houses lie in earthquake zones.

Much of the housing in such zones — especially the eastern Mediterranean and much of Latin America — consists of such things as heavy adobe (mud) block or stone and timber walls with stone, mud or heavy timber roofs. Such buildings "are about the worst possible for an earthquake area", according to Tony Waltham. The vulnerability of heavy Third World houses has been a subject of controversy among the technical experts, as few such houses have been connected to measuring devices and subjected to stress. Yet after quakes in such countries as Turkey, Yemen, Iran, Guatemala, Nicaragua and Colombia, a great many victims are found crushed beneath the remains of their houses.

At the Seventh World Conference on Earthquake Engineering in Istanbul in 1980, a group of six leading engineering seismologists from India, Italy, Yugoslavia, Mexico, Peru and China reported on their studies of risk to rural structures. They note in their "state of the art" report:

> "It is unfortunate that this risk is increasing, rather than decreasing in most places on account of an increasing population, poverty of the people, scarcity of wood, cement and steel, lack of understanding of earthquake-resistant features, etc." They also noted that "the number of dwelling units may double in the next 20-25 years due to the explosion of populations in developing countries."

When Ian Davis of Oxford Polytechnic (UK) visited the earthquake-prone area of Karakoram in northern Pakistan, he found substantial houses with heavy walls of timber baulks interspersed with dry masonry. They were fairly resistant to quakes, but when they did fall they became death traps for those inside. Davis was more surprised to find that the construction of the new buildings of reinforced concrete being put up both privately and by the government was "likely to be inferior to the traditional construction it has replaced", and more vulnerable to earthquakes. Part of the problem is the migration from rural areas of skilled builders bound for the major cities of Pakistan or even for the richer Gulf states.

The Karakoram traditional houses were more vulnerable because of where they were built rather than how they were built. Many were constructed against the vertical sides of mountains, in the line of landslides, of rockfalls (whether caused by quakes or floods or other factors) and of floods. The people realised their vulnerability, but preferred to build here rather than on the little available open agricultural land.

Similar problems exist in Central America and the Andes, where much of the housing is of heavy adobe which can fall and kill residents. Also many houses in this region are built on narrow ledges, against the sides of the hills or mountains behind and with steep drops in front. Some houses are not built on flat ledges but on steep slopes. During a quake they can be thrown down the mountain. Of course, they are also more vulnerable to floods and avalanches.

Printed advice by relief agencies to those rebuilding after the 1976 Guatemala earthquake showed a man standing stretching his arms, one hand barely touching the house and the other the mountain side. This indicated the minimum space to be left between house and mountainside. The drawing also showed ample room between the house and the edge of the slope in front, and it depicted the hillside behind the new house as having been terraced. This good advice presupposes that the family in question have a housing plot big enough to leave the proper safety margins.

Much Third World urban housing is also vulnerable to earthquakes. Few developing countries have skilled people to spare to check that building codes have been followed by builders. Government wages for such work tend to be low, leaving such officials susceptible to bribes.

Large urban apartment blocks are dangerous when they have poor foundations — whether too shallow, on poorly compacted fill or underconsolidated sediments. Substandard concrete or steel may be used, or the building simply badly designed. Waltham points out that many buildings failed in the 1963 Skopje Yugoslavia earthquake (6.0 Richter, over 1,000 dead) because of a poor bind between concrete on unwashed aggregate. Other multi-storey buildings there "pancaked" into heaps of rubble because good reinforced concrete floors were separated by unreinforced masonry walls. Much of the damage in the 1930 Italian quake was caused by heavy rounded stones used in buildings.

Following the 1977 Romanian quake (1,400 dead), President Ceauşescu gave a rare press interview in which he expressed the hope of credits from the United States to build earthquake-proof buildings. He noted that many modern structures had collapsed in the quake, and promised that their designers and architects would be prosecuted for violating building codes.

In 1954, El Asnam, Algeria, suffered an earthquake in which 1,600 people died. The French rebuilt the destroyed buildings with "earthquake-proof" architecture. Another quake struck El Asnam in 1980, killing some 3,600 people, leaving 300,000 homeless, damaging 80% of the buildings and completely destroying 25%. Angry officials noted that the most damaged buildings were the "quake-proof" structures built by the French.

Earthquakes or classquakes?

Strictly-enforced building codes and zoning laws make Northern earthquake-prone cities less and less vulnerable. As discussed in the section on urban floods in Chapter Three, a growing number of people are building their own homes in Third World cities on illegally occupied land. They are outside any building or zoning regulations. In the rural countryside virtually no building or zoning regulations exist. Building codes, land use, zoning and urban and regional planning techniques "have had no impact on reducing vulnerability in the Third World. For the most part, zoning and building codes are unenforceable", notes US disaster expert Frederick Cuny.

Of all disasters, an earthquake would appear at first glance to be no respecter of social class, affecting rich and poor equally. But the 1976 Guatemala earthquake seemed to almost seek out the poor. How did this happen?

The Guatemala quake (Richter 7.5) killed 22,000, injured 75,000 and left over one million of the nation's six million people without shelter. Most of the damage was north and west of Guatemala City and along the Montagua River running eastwards into the Atlantic Ocean. Some 9,100 square kilometres (3,500 sq miles) of the most densely populated part of the country were affected. Fourteen towns were almost totally destroyed. In another 17 towns, less than one-third of the buildings were left standing.

It was the poor who died in the rural highlands because it is the poor who live in the rural highlands. But in the capital:

> "Some 1,200 people died and 90,000 were made homeless in Guatemala City, almost exclusively in the slum areas of the city. In this well-known fault zone the houses of the rich have been built to costly anti-earthquake specifications. Most of the poorest housing, on the other hand, is in the ravines or gorges which are highly susceptible to landslides whenever earth movements occur" (the journal *Latin America,* 9 April 1976).

The poor also suffered for more obvious political reasons. The city was governed by the most radical opposition tolerated in Guatemala, the Frente Unido de la Revolución, a social democratic coalition. So the more conservative national government passed along a disproportionately small amount of the aid to the city. The Front's leader was shot and killed by unknown gunmen within two months of the quake, and another party official was shot down two weeks after the quake after he suggested that the homeless should be allowed to rebuild on unoccupied private land.

The 1972 Managua, Nicaragua, earthquake registered 6.2 on the Richter scale and killed 5,000 people; the 1971 quake in the much more developed community of San Fernando, California, registered 6.6 on the Richter but killed only 65. Some $800 million worth of property was lost in Managua, $535 million in San Fernando, but US disaster expert Robert Kates reckoned that these losses had 15 times the economic impact on the poorer economy of Nicaragua.

Other major Third World cities in which large numbers of the poor are forced to live on dangerous ground in dangerous structures include Lima, Santiago, Quito, Guayaquil and Caracas.

The 1976 Guatemala earthquake. Almost all of the 1,200 people which the quake killed in Guatemala City lived in the capital's slums and shantytowns.

Governments face a choice of acknowledging the presence of illegal shantytowns by providing sanitation, water and road programmes — and thus being seen to abet the lawbreakers — or of constantly demolishing shantytowns, which would mean a continual war against the poor. So many governments compromise by officially ignoring their presence. Thus it was largely the outside aid agencies, both private concerns such as OXFAM and government agencies such as the US Agency for International Development, which worked with the homeless after the Guatemala quake and showed them simple ways of making their houses safer. These measures included corrugated iron roof sheeting, timber frames for adobe, braces for the corners and even chicken wire to keep adobe from tumbling inwards. (For a further discussion of housing after quakes, see Chapter Eight).

Prediction: the high technology approach

Given the messy social problems which arise over the earthquake vulnerability of the poor, it is no wonder that most earthquake experts prefer to work in the more scientifically precise field of earthquake prediction. Western science has achieved no prediction worthy of the name, but then given the relatively short time during which the basic theory of plate tectonics has been widely held, this is not surprising.

If an earthquake is the result of a sudden release of stored up energy, then one ought to be able to find a way to measure the energy in "storage" and the ability of the rock system to store it and then name the time the sudden release will come. But so far this line of thinking has led only to vague notions that certain parts of the world are "due". Many US seismologists certainly feel that the San Andreas fault has been too quiet for too long. "If a repeat of the 1906 earthquake hit San Francisco today, at least 2,000 people, and maybe more than 100,000 would die", writes British geologist Tony Waltham. "The figure would largely depend on the time of day and the number of dam failures. But another earthquake in San Francisco is a certainty. The city lies on one of the world's most active faults, and it will move again — sometime in the not too distant future."

Lisbon has had major quakes in 1344, 1531 and 1755 — intervals of about 200 years which indicate that another major event is due there. Parts of the Caribbean are also "overdue". But none of this number-divining can be called "prediction".

US experts have a wealth of seismic equipment to measure various tiny shocks, and laser beams to measure slight changes in ground level. A mass of data has been gathered, but the experts can only debate what the data means. For instance, seismologists had been carefully measuring an area of 13,000 sq km (5,000 sq miles) around Palmdale, California, which slowly rose over 1959-74. It was thought that the swelling "Palmdale Bulge" heralded a quake. But the bulge stopped rising in 1974, and there has been no reasonable explanation for its stability since.

The best apparent advance in prediction comes from the Russians. They found that before a quake the ratio of the speeds of the P and S waves change. The P waves slow down, apparently because rocks are fracturing during dilation, but then speed up again just before a quake as water flows into the fractures. Measurements released by Soviet scientists for two Soviet quakes show impressively similar curves in wave ratios. US, Chinese and Japanese seismologists have verified these results, and claim successful "predictions" in areas covered with enough seismographs. But the time-scale of such predictions is in weeks, and the findings have yet to lead to predictions which have saved lives.

Soviet scientists are also investigating gases, especially the heavy gas radon, which they believe are squeezed out of rocks before a quake. They have found higher concentrations of radon in well water before a seismic event.

In 1978, academician A.G. Babaev, president of the Turkmen Academy of Sciences, USSR, claimed a month after the event to have forecasted the earthquake at Tabas, Iran, in which at least 25,000 people were killed. The Soviet scientists said they made this forecast 10-15 days before the quake occurred. "We felt an earthquake was going to occur", said Babaev, but the Turkmen scientists were clearly embarrassed when asked to say how accurately they had been able to forecast its time, location, and intensity, and their replies may well have played down their degree of foreknowledge. Sudden changes in groundwater levels and slope near Ashkhabad were the warning signs. "We expected it within some days", said Babaev. "Its epicentre could be forecasted only within a circle of 1,000 km (620 miles) radius, and we could not be sure whether it would be within Iran or the USSR."

The National Meteorological Agency of Japan, a nation which registers some 10,000 earthquakes per year (most of them too mild to be felt by humans), has about 150 earthquake monitoring stations, but it has made no great strides in predicting.

Greece is experimenting with a warning system which involves placing two iron rods in the ground and monitoring variations in the electronic fields between them. The system is based on indications that there is a marked change in such fields six to eight hours before an earthquake. Combining data from several monitoring stations, manned constantly by young men as an alternative to military service, has led to impressive predictions of the time, location and magnitude of quakes, according to Swedish seismologists advising the programme. But the work has yet to be rigorously evaluated, and it is controversial in Greece because it is led by physicists rather than seismologists.

China's peasant predictors

In the late 1970s China claimed to have predicted 18 out of 31 recent earthquakes. China had decided in 1966 to "mobilise the masses" to spot the warning signs. These warning signs had little to do with seismographs, but instead concerned common countryside events such as the behaviour of animals and the level of water in wells. (However, the Chinese have also been measuring radon emissions.)

In 1970 a "gap" was noticed in earthquake activity in the densely populated, industrialised province of Liaoning in northeast China. The area was carefully watched. There were small quakes, and then on 1 February 1975, seismic activity fell off sharply. By this time there were several thousand amateur earthquake experts ready and waiting. On the afternoon of 4 February a number of cities in the province were ordered to be evacuated, including the city of Haicheng. Outdoor movies were shown to get people into the countryside. Later that afternoon a quake (Richter 7.3) spread damage across 1,000 sq km (386 sq miles) and wrecked 90% of the city of Haicheng. Casualty figures were not given but were described as "minimal loss of life".

Signs the amateur Chinese seismologists watch for include chickens roosting in trees, fish leaping out of the water in large numbers, horses refusing to enter stalls, snakes leaving the ground, dogs howling and other animals acting nervously. The Chinese believe the bat is the animal most sensitive to approaching earthquakes; the Japanese hold with the pheasant. Well water is also believed to rise before a quake. These homely signals are collated over a sophisticated information gathering network linking regional centres.

Several theories have been put forward as to why animals are sensitive to approaching earthquakes, if indeed they are. Stress on rocks may cause them to emit sounds above or below the range of human hearing. Fowls' legs may be sensitive to vibrations. Some animals may be able to detect the changes in the earth's magnetic field believed to take place before a quake.

The Chinese admit to false alarms, which are more acceptable in a disciplined country than in Northern democracies where people would doubtless sue over lost income and mental stress. (Some Western critics of the Chinese approach claim that there have been as many as 40 false alarms in China in the past decade.) Two years after the successful Liaoning prediction came the Tangshan quake (Richter 7.6) with its official death toll of 242,000. Long and medium-term indicators had raised fears of a quake there; but either short-term indications were missed, or there were none.

There are fears in the less orderly North that a government earthquake warning could cause more damage and even loss of life than an earthquake. Psychologists at the University of Colorado's Institute of Behavioral Sciences consulted residents of a California earthquake zone and found that unless education and other preparations were begun soon, the first credible earthquake prediction "will exact a very high price in economic dislocation and social disruption".

In the five years up to 1983, the Chinese government had spent some $100 million reinforcing existing buildings in quake-prone cities, but China remained far behind the US and Japan in building against quakes. In 1984, UN experts hoped to finish installing a complex programme of digital sensors in northeast China. Yet no one was sure that the data collected would help: "No one has a computer programme that you can plug in and which will say, 'Here's your next big earthquake'", UN development official Joseph Meyer told *Newsweek* magazine.

Induce-and-control

Several times this century, humans have accidentally caused earthquakes, and these experiences have given scientists hope of controlling quakes in the future.

As Lake Mead in Arizona was filled behind the Boulder Dam in 1935, there were 600 shocks up to 5.0 on the Richter scale. The filling of the Koyna reservoir near Bombay in 1967 seemed to trigger many shocks, including one of 6.5 magnitude which killed 177 people. Such quakes are apparently caused both by the weight of water on the rocks and by an increase in groundwater pressure which "lubricates" the rocks. The city of Ashkhabad in the Central Asian Soviet republic of Turkmenistan suffers an incredible 1,000 "quakes" per year — most of them sensed only by instruments. In the mid-1970s there were fears in the city that bringing water from the distant Pamir Mountains via the Lenin Canal into the area would increase quakes, but there has been no evidence that the fears were realised.

There are also theories that the frequency of small tremors found in some mountain areas of the world, particularly the Himalayas, are caused by the increasing amounts of water coming off the mountains due to deforestation.

Between 1962 and 1968 there were some 610 small quakes around Denver, Colorado, where there had been virtually none before. Investigations found that since 1962, fluid waste from the manufacture of nerve gas had been pumped into the fractured granite at the bottom of deep wells, and that the tremors started within seven weeks of this pumping. (When the source of the tremors was recognised, the pumping was stopped.) Petroleum engineers had also noticed that pumping water into oil wells to extract the last bit of oil caused an increase in seismic activity. In 1969, seismographs were set up in a Colorado oil field when water was injected, and a dramatic increase in seismic activity was measured. Three years later, the water was pumped out, and the tremors ceased.

Such observations have caused seismologists to dream of controlling earthquake faults as if they were long zippers across the face of the Earth. A fault could be "locked" at two points by pumping water from the ground. At a point between the two locks, water could be pumped in, and a mild earthquake induced, releasing tension in the fault. Humans could choose when and where to hold earthquakes. Perhaps even the magnitudes of these quakes could also be controlled.

An underground nuclear test in Nevada in 1968, which itself registered 6.3 on the Richter scale, was followed by a series of tremors up to 5.0. This event suggests that nuclear devices could also be used to trigger "controlled" earthquakes.

But it is not immediately clear what part water and nuclear devices can play in saving Los Angeles or San Francisco, much less Guatemala City or Managua.

Geology or psychology?

Much discussion of earthquake mitigation assumes that humans make logical decisions in the face of risks.

As British geologist Tony Waltham notes, the path of the active Hayward

Fault — a branch of the San Andreas Fault — as it passes through the city of Oakland, California, has been well known for some time. But 14 schools, two hospitals and a massive football stadium have been built across it. This happened in a nation where zoning and building regulations are relatively carefully considered and strictly enforced.

In 1959, the US Geological Survey described the potential danger from quakes in certain areas of Anchorage, Alaska, over sensitive clay. But houses and a school were later built on the exact locations. During the 1964 quake they crumbled, and the press described it as a "tragedy". The Alaska quake killed 100 people; and the US National Academy of Sciences has devoted $20 million to a study of it, which was published in nine volumes.

India has built a rock-filled dam at the confluence of the Bhagirathi and Bhilangana Rivers in Uttar Pradesh state in a seismically active area. There will be some three billion tonnes of water behind the dam.

Landslides (usually associated more with floods, hillside clearance and unsound development, rather than earthquakes) cause $1.5 billion in property losses and about 25 deaths each year in the United States. This monetary loss is greater than the combined losses from floods, earthquakes, hurricanes and tornadoes. Yet 25 rapidly expanding metropolitan areas are built in landslide zones. William Kockelman of the US Geological Survey argues: "Information on hazardous geological processes is not being obtained, transmitted or used at a rate that keeps pace with current development. Landslide damage continues year after year, but only major catastrophes attract worldwide attention."

If this is true for the United States, to what extent can science be relied on to mitigate geological disasters in the Third World?

Chapter 6

Tsunami and volcanoes

"Whenever I look at a mountain I always expect
it to turn into a volcano."
Italo Svevo, *Confessions of Zeno* (Italy, 1923)

Though it makes little difference to those submerged by them, so-called "tidal waves" have little to do with tides. They are properly called seismic sea waves, but are better known by their Japanese name, "tsunami".

The 19th century British engineer Robert Mallet, one of the world's first "seismologists", correctly guessed that such waves are caused by underwater land slippages, as in an earthquake. They can also be caused by inland earthquakes and volcanic eruptions.

The 1883 Krakatoa eruption sent tsunami into the East Indies coasts, killing an estimated 36,000. The Lisbon quake caused a rise in tide of 3.6 metres (12 feet), some 5,474 km (3,400 miles) away in Antigua in the Caribbean.

But most tsunami — almost always a series of waves rather than just one — are connected with vertical undersea earth displacements such as occur in the faults along the coasts of Japan, South America and the Aleutian Islands (off Alaska). California's faults move horizontally, so do not generate these massive waves. The Pacific is the most dangerous tsunami area, but the world's deadliest such event killed an estimated 200,000 people along India's densely populated Bengal coast in 1876.

In the deep open ocean, tsunami travel at about 700 kph (435 mph), and are very low, so that they often pass large ships unnoticed. As they approach the shallow waters near shore, they slow down and become much higher. The waves themselves can be 480 km (300 miles) long. Japan's worst tsunami, the result of an undersea quake about 150 km (93 miles) offshore, killed 27,000 people in 1897 on the Sanriku coast of northern Honshu Island. Fishermen far out to sea did not notice the waves passing beneath their boats. But upon their return they found their villages destroyed.

In the summer of 1983, Japan was surprised by a tsunami out of the Sea of Japan, an area which normally suffers few quakes. However, a quake — its epicentre 160 km (100 miles) offshore and registering 7.7 on the Richter scale — shook buildings, cracked roads, twisted rails and destroyed at least 400 homes. Yet most of the damage and the death toll of over 100 was caused by 1.5-3 metre (5-10 feet) tsunami waves which battered the north coast of

Mark Edwards/Earthscan

A Haitian seafront. People living on gently sloping shores where houses have replaced vegetation are more vulnerable both to tsunamis and the storm surges of cyclones. The Caribbean has suffered 22 major tsunamis betwen 1530 and 1969.

Japan for over eight hours. Many of the dead were workmen thrown from breakwaters as the waves rushed up rivers. The waves were also felt on the eastern coast of South Korea 965 km (600 miles) away.

Tsunami work their destruction in complex ways. Some come crashing over seaside settlements like large breakers, 25-30 metres (80-100 feet) high, the weight of water crushing the buildings, perhaps hurling ships and seaside structures onto buildings further inland. Other tsunami may cause the water to rise gently over a village, floating the buildings off their foundations. But then the violent backwash may sweep buildings and people out to sea. The force of a tsunami which wrecked much of Hilo, Hawaii, and killed 159 people in 1946 bent parking meters double. That tsunami — eight waves in all — originated near the Aleutian Islands.

Peter Verney, a writer on quakes and related matters, describes a "typical" tsunami on the western coast of Latin America. First comes "the smooth one", in which the sea gently rises beyond the high tide mark. This is followed by a violent sucking sound as the sea retreats, leaving rocks, reefs and sunken ships exposed, and anchored ships on dry ground. Out to sea the water seems to bump and boil like whales at play. Then with a huge roar comes a wave at a speed of up to 200 kph (125 mph) — depending on the slope of the coast — sweeping everything before it. The water may remain high for 10-15 minutes or longer. Then with a great sucking noise it withdraws, taking wreckage out to sea. Following waves, moving at slower speeds, "come to finish the job". Where villages are built at the head of a gradually narrowing bay or inlet, as are many fishing villages around the world, the tsunami generate more height and more destructive force.

Warn and avoid

Following the 1946 Hilo tsunami, a communications network covering all the Pacific Ocean nations was established to warn of the giant waves.

The "Pacific Tsunami Warning System" can be effective for waves moving across broad bodies of water, as it may take 10 hours for a wave to travel from Japan to Hawaii. But it is of little help to coastal areas near an undersea quake's epicentre.

In 1960, one of the world's more powerful quakes struck south-central Chile and sent tsunami off across the Pacific. The waves' arrival time in Hawaii was quickly calculated, and, 15 hours after the quake, they struck Hawaii, within a minute of the calculated time, according to British vulcanologist Peter Francis. When the waves — one 10 metres (33 feet) high — struck Hilo they killed 62 people who had chosen to ignore the warnings, perhaps because the tsunami which followed previous warnings had been insignificant, Francis speculates. When the waves struck Japan 22 hours after the quake, also on schedule, 180 people died.

After the powerful 1964 Alaskan quake, a tsunami warning went out to Crescent City in northern California. People moved back from the beaches; two waves struck, and some people returned. Many of these were drowned by more powerful third and fourth waves. British geologist Tony Waltham notes that television warnings in San Francisco actually drew people to the beaches to "watch the waves", which fortunately were not serious in the area.

Undersea quakes release other waves besides tsunami. A sound wave, occasionally heard on ships and detectable by instruments, arrives before the tsunami (2.5 hours in the case of Crescent City), and scientists hope these can be used as part of a warning system. The quakes also bounce a little-understood wave off the ionosphere (which reflects radio waves), and this too may help provide an early warning.

Tsunami are relatively rare events. One of the world's most vulnerable areas, the east coast of Honshu, receives an average of one locally destructive tsunami once every 10 years.

Little account of tsunami is taken in deciding where and how to build. Waltham notes that in the rebuilding after the 1946 Hilo disaster some areas of the foreshore were left undeveloped. "But short of depopulating half the Pacific coast, the hazards of tsunamis in the area must be accepted as a part of life", he concludes.

Nevertheless, the destruction of seafront dunes, coral reefs and mangroves and other forests adds to the vulnerability of villages behind such natural defences.

The Munich Reinsurance Company found in 1982: "Exposure is limited to the regions directly around the coast, in exceptional cases to areas about 1 km (0.6 miles) inland. The fact that more and more industrial plants and rows of hotels are being built around the coast means that the tsunami exposure has recently become much more significant."

Volcanoes

Volcanic eruptions are not "serious" disasters in terms of global numbers of people killed, or even affected.

The 1902 eruption of Mt Pelee on the island of Martinique killed some 29,000 people — virtually everyone in the city of St Pierre. That eruption killed more people than all the other volcanoes in the world this century.

But what volcanoes lack in death tolls they make up for in awesome spectacle. And they will cause major calamities in the future, just as they have done in the past. The eruption of Santorini in the Aegean Sea around 1470 BC is thought to have changed the development of Western civilisation by wiping out the Minoan Culture of Crete. An eruption of Mt Etna in Sicily in 1669 killed 20,000 people. When the Laki fissure erupted in Iceland in 1783, so much ash covered croplands that most of the 10,000 people — a fifth of the nation's population — listed as victims of the eruption died of famine, as did hundreds of thousands of sheep. The eruption in 1815 of Temboro in Indonesia and the tsunami it caused killed 56,000. The 1883 eruption of Krakatoa off the west coast of Java, Indonesia and the subsequent tsunami killed over 36,000. This formed the basis of the film which Hollywood perversely called *Krakatoa — East of Java*.

"All around our over-crowded world there are potentially dangerous volcanoes with tens of thousands of people living on their flanks", writes Peter Francis. "It is inescapable that volcanic eruptions are bound to take place in the future, and as population pressure around the world increases, more and more people are bound to be affected by them."

One of the simplest ways to avoid death by eruption is to avoid proximity to volcanoes. But in fact people tend to crowd around them to take advantage of the rich volcanic soil, high in potassium. In the tropics, especially in rainforest areas where other soils are poor, volcanoes may provide the only rich soils in a nation. In Indonesia, maps of population density neatly coincide with maps of past and sometimes present volcanic activity; such soils can

Jean-Michel Goudstikker/International Red Cross

In 1983, more than 300 eruptions by the Indonesian volcano Galunggung covered fields with ashes and then flooded them by filling rivers with debris and boulders. But volcanoes have given Indonesia much of its richest soil, and people crowd around them.

provide two or three crops per year. Costa Rica and Guatemala claim that their best coffee is grown on volcanic slopes. Volcanic soils provide the basis of much of Hawaii's rich agriculture.

Peter Francis proves the attraction of volcanoes by citing the history of Taal volcano, on an island just offshore in Lake Taal south of the city of Manila in the Philippines. The mountain has erupted regularly, but for much of its history has caused a small number of deaths as few people lived near it. A 1754 eruption killed 12 people. Population increased despite the regular warnings. A 1911 eruption killed almost all 500 people living on the island and 800 onshore. The survivors had nowhere else to go, so resettled around the lake, and even on the island. A violent eruption in 1965 was preceded by warnings and a partial evacuation, so only 190 people died. Within a few days of the 1965 blast people moved back onto their plots to begin again, writes Francis, "no doubt hoping that the next eruption would not come in their lifetimes. Unfortunately, though, there is every possibility that Taal will erupt again within the lifetime of some of them..."

In 79 AD an eruption of Mt Vesuvius buried the cities of Pompeii and

Herculaneum in western Italy. The mountain has erupted several times since then (1631, 1794, 1906) but not violently. But as Francis points out, population densities around the mountain today are many times greater than they were in Roman times, so a major eruption could be much more disastrous.

Problems are compounded by the fact that a great many dangerous volcanoes are on islands, with fairly high population densities around them. Such islands — large and small — include Krakatoa, Java, Iceland, Hawaii and Sicily.

Volcanoes are found on almost every one of the islands in the Lesser Antilles islands of the Caribbean. On some small islands, virtually 100% of the population are vulnerable to an eruption — 12,000 people on Nevis, and on Saba and St Eustatius about 1,300 each. The population of St Pierre, Martinique, at about 6,000, is much lower than before the 1902 eruption. But capital cities such as Bassetarre in Guadeloupe, Roseau in Dominica, and Plymouth in Montserrat all have growing populations on the flanks of potentially dangerous volcanoes.

Predicting and containing

A volcanic eruption is both spectacular and very complicated. Eruptions come in many varieties, and the types of matter spewed from a volcano take many forms.

Lava flows which are not too massive, and which have not reached valleys carved out by previous flows, can sometimes be contained or guided by earth barriers erected by bulldozers. These were partly successful in the 1955 and 1960 eruptions of Kilauea in Hawaii. Directing water at a lava flow can cool its front, slow it and even stop it; this was first tried in Hawaii. During the 1973 eruption of Helgafjell on the island of Heimey off Iceland, high pressure streams of water impeded lava, saving buildings and preventing the lava from filling in the entrance of Iceland's largest fishing port.

Bombing or blasting lava flows has had mixed results almost everywhere it has been tried, from the first attempts on Mt Etna in 1669. Here explosions were used to split streams of lava, and a canal was dug to redirect the new stream. Similar attempts were made on Etna lava flows in 1983, but the results remain controversial. Bombers of the US Army Air Corps attacked lava flows from Mauna Loa volcano in 1935, which were threatening the city of Hilo in Hawaii. The lava flow stopped completely, but no one is quite sure why. Similar raids were made against Mauna Loa lava flows in 1942, but on this occasion the lava stopped naturally, with the bombs having little effect.

More dangerous than lava in eruptions are the more rapidly moving mudflows and "nuées ardantes" (French for "glowing clouds"). It was such a glowing cloud that flattened the city of St Pierre in Martinique to such an extent that post-eruption photos show a collection of low walls which resembles a part of a city vaporised by the direct strike of an atomic bomb.

US vulcanologist Frank Perret described these hot avalanches as dense masses of hot, highly gas-charged and constantly gas-emitting fragmental lava. They can move at speeds of up to 100 kph (60 mph) as the particles are almost frictionless, each being separated from its neighbour by a cushion of compressed gas. No way has been yet devised to contain such a nuée ardante.

Mudflows are another uncontainable effect of volcanoes. The term is misleading, as the flow which comes down the mountain at avalanche speed contains every sort of material from fine sand to huge rocks. An eruption is not necessary for a mudflow, as monsoon rains can release lava and ash fragments on the side of a volcano and cause a disaster. "Hot" mudflows occur when an eruption shoots up through a crater lake, sending down the mountain a mixture of boiling water and debris approaching the speeds of nuées ardantes.

This phenomenon is notorious in Indonesia, where mudflows from the Kelut volcano killed 5,000 people in 1919. A series of tunnels were later dug to drain the lake in the centre of the volcano. A 1951 eruption of Kelut did not produce a mudflow but did wreck the drainage system. A 1966 eruption caused mudflows which killed several hundred people and the drainage system was improved.

Ash falls cannot be diverted, but their effects can be minimised by the simple expedient of building steeply sloping roofs on houses near volcanoes. British vulcanologist Peter Francis notes that during a 1906 eruption of Mt Vesuvius the villagers of San Giuseppe took shelter in their village church, and many were killed when the weight of the ash caused the church roof to collapse. Had the villagers stayed home and shovelled the ash off their own roofs, they could have saved their lives and property.

Vulcanologists are confident that they will soon be able to predict eruptions by measuring the heat of the mountain with infra-red aerial photos; by measuring the change in the magnetic properties of the mountains as the rocks inside heat up; or by measuring the changing "tilt" of the slope by a "tiltmeter" — a series of water-filled tubes only slightly more complex than a carpenter's spirit level. There are even grand plans for placing sensors on many particularly dangerous volcanoes (in terms of activity or vulnerable populations), and using orbiting satellites to regularly collect the data these sensors produce.

Chapter 7

Relief

"To these from birth is Relief forbidden;
from these till death is Relief afar."
Rudyard Kipling
(Late 19th century Anglo-Indian writer)

It may appear churlish to question the value of international relief after a natural disaster. We have become familiar with problems connected with military aid, long-term food aid and even much development aid. By comparison, disaster relief — getting food, medicine and shelter to populations suddenly bereft of these things — seems like benign and selfless charity.

But it is becoming more and more doubtful, say growing numbers of relief experts and field workers, whether relief is a cost-effective operation in terms of the best way to spend a given amount of money to help the afflicted people. Some disaster relief is being planned and managed on the basis of incorrect assumptions and mixed political and economic motives. These doubts about relief are only slowly percolating into the consciousness of the general public. They are in fact felt most strongly in the collective minds of the relief agencies themselves. For it is these agencies which must cope with the growing flood of disaster appeals from the poorer developing nations. The relief agencies are coming to realise that emergency relief by itself is no longer an adequate response.

The following chapter is not meant to be an attack on relief. Yet documenting as it does many of the ways well-intended relief schemes can go wrong, it may sound like such. In many disasters, nothing but relief is possible, due perhaps to warfare or to regimes which will not accept long-term development assistance and instead insist on short-term, emergency aid.

Relief work is steadily more difficult, not only from the point of view of deciding whether or to what extent intervention in a disaster which has both "natural" and "political" causes, but also from the point of view of basic logistics — getting material effectively to the field. Third World disasters have reached such overwhelming proportions that foreign disaster assistance, even if efficiently planned and organised, can play only a marginal role in mitigating them. Relief work today is like bandaging a wound that is constantly growing.

Third World disasters — particularly droughts and floods, the two which are increasing most rapidly — will demand increasing amounts of international attention in the future. Traditional relief will continue to be a major part of the international response. But to at least slow the rate of increase in disasters, governments and aid donors will have to recognise the human hand in causing these catastrophes, and stop treating each disaster only as a logistical exercise in moving men and equipment. Whenever possible, short-term assistance should be linked to longer-term improvements aimed at disaster prevention.

Thus in critically analysing some aspects of relief assistance in its more traditional forms, the following chapter does not mean to question the value of relief itself in all cases, but to point out the need for improvements in execution and for a redefinition of the basic objectives of relief operations.

The helplessness myth

Despite constant debunking, the prevailing image of disaster victims is of a huddled mass of dazed humanity, deep in shock after the initial panic has worn off.

However, one of the key findings of the US National Opinion Research Council's 1950-54 research into human behaviour in disasters was that panic and other forms of uncontrolled behaviour were relatively rare. In 1953, the US National Academy of Sciences (NAS) became interested in disasters and formed a Disaster Research Group which worked in the field until 1963. During its 10 years of study, it divided disasters into various "phases" and examined how people acted in each.

It found that during the *impact phase* there was virtually no panic. Ad hoc leaders tended to emerge who had no tested leadership ability but who had skills to offer which were needed in the situation. In the *inventory phase* immediately following impact, people engaged in search and rescue activities and sought family and friends. Social coordination gave way to loose, informal organisational structures among and within groups.

In the *rescue phase* some people became docile or passive, a condition which rendered them more receptive to suggestions and authority, but this phase tended to be restricted to really large disasters in which there had been great disruption and destruction. During the *remedy phase* there was a heightening of interaction between individuals and groups, with class barriers breaking down and outside relief groups being ostracised by the stricken community.

These NAS findings have remained disputed, and in the early 1960s some researchers were attacking the entire disaster research field as being politically controversial, empirically weak and experimentally difficult. Nevertheless, the early work did a lot to dispel myths — myths which have needed repeated dispelling ever since. The League of Red Cross Societies' *Disaster Relief Handbook,* published in 1976 and still in use in early 1984, carried the following definition of "disaster":

"A disaster is a catastrophic situation in which the day-to-day patterns of life are — in many instances — suddenly disrupted and people are plunged into helplessness and suffering and, as a result, need protection, food, clothing, shelter, medical and social care, and other necessities of life."

(A new edition of the handbook was being prepared, in which the definition of "disaster" did not use the word "helplessness".)

Ian Davis, a director of the Evangelican Alliance Relief Fund, a lecturer in architecture at Oxford Polytechnic, UK, and an expert in housing after disasters, attacked the "helplessness myth" again recently, and gave some hints as to why it persists. He said of agencies which intervene in foreign disasters:

"The activity into which they intrude is the local ad hoc process that takes place after every disaster. This is the way a given Third World society buries its dead, cares for its wounded, clears the debris and eventually rebuilds its homes.

The entire local process is very rarely referred to in the foreign media's coverage of disasters. Their focus is normally on external aid. As a direct result the average Western reader has a false image — one of dazed or panicking individuals totally unable to cope with their crisis, waiting anxiously for the helicopters to bring them outside help.

This picture is supported by the publicity that emerges from the relief agencies. For very obvious reasons they maximise their role, and by implication minimise the local role of people satisfying their own needs. This may be a subconscious process of reporting but there is no doubt it colours the majority of the information reaching the Western public.

In fact survivors are very unlikely to be in a state of shock or exhibit signs of panic. They normally act with calm precision using their common sense.

Unless there are exceptional mitigating circumstances such as famine, they will not wait for aid to arrive before taking individual action. For example, external help in rebuilding seldom amounts to more than 20% of the homes constructed."

Experience shows that it is always the victims who bear the brunt of work and expense in providing their own post-disaster relief. According to US disaster consultant Frederick Cuny, foreign disaster aid has never covered more than 40% of the costs of relief in a Third World disaster. In many cases it covers a much smaller proportion.

The office of the UN Disaster Relief Co-ordinator (UNDRO) noted in its 1982 report *Shelter After Disaster* that "often, far from being dazed and distraught by the loss of their homes, the survivors are amazingly resilient — the best resource for reconstruction". It advised relief workers to harness this resource.

One flood, one village

In 1983, Orissa state on India's east coast suffered massive flooding. An independent, non-profit, development-oriented group called Unnayan based in Calcutta, which has done a great deal of work on disasters, sent a study team to the village of Balisahi, which had just been inundated by the normally placid Prachi River.

When the floods came, the villagers grabbed what items they could and ran to a nearby raised road. When waters covered the road, they walked down it several hundred metres to a small rise where, with victims from other villages, they built shelters. As the waters receded, they moved back nearer the village, but had to build shelters again on the road, as most of their post-and-thatch houses had collapsed. There was no panic, no helplessness. People lived in the shelters for 10-14 days after the flood. Many women and children received aid in a nearby school, an effort organised by a voluntary relief committee set up by the residents of an unaffected village across the river. A larger but still voluntary agency based in the nearby city of Puri then helped out.

The research team found that within 14 days after the height of the floods, some of the villagers had already built houses for themselves, and others were in the process of building. No government agent had visited the village, whether to provide relief or to check on damage in order to sanction housing grants automatically provided for in the Orissa Relief Code. So none of the builders had received grants, according to a report in the Indian journal *Disaster Management,* April-June 1983.

The Unnayan study said: "In order for any reconstruction aid to be useful, it is essential that provision should start within 10-20 days of the disaster, so that the support is according to the reconstruction timetable of the survivors, not of outside agencies". But few people had received any help three weeks after the June cyclones. "Beyond a certain period of time, it is questionable whether 'aid' can even be called aid; or whether it is more of a nuisance, a confusing factor.... Current research into post-flood housing reconstruction, in India and in other parts of the world, is increasingly showing that the practice of the people of Balisahi is almost universal", the Unnayan report argued.

There was in fact one "helpless" group in Balisahi: the poorest, those of the lowest or "untouchable" caste (the Harijans). However, their helplessness stemmed not from the flood but from previous efforts by outsiders to help them. After floods in 1980, the government had built them brick houses with asbestos roofs. In the 1983 floods, many of these houses had collapsed and their roofs split. The poor lacked the money, materials and skills to rebuild their brick houses; besides, they were waiting for the government to build them, as they had before. They were not told that the state chief minister had declared that this time there would be no such housing aid. He did not explain whether this was because the flooding was too extensive or whether such housing had been judged a misguided expenditure, as many critics had charged. Thus the only helpless victims were as much victims of previous intervention as of the flood.

Relief as intervention

On a normal day-to-day basis, a Third World community — whether a nation, city or shantytown — is an extremely complex network of deals, debts, kinships and relationships. During a disaster these relationships do not vanish; they aid the recovery and rebuilding processes. Thus it is not an easy task for relief agencies from other lands and other cultures to bring into such complicated systems goods and advice which are appropriate and helpful.

"Agencies repeatedly attempt to simplify what is a complex process; and by doing so, they create innumerable problems, not only for themselves, but also for the society which they are trying to assist", writes US disaster consultant Frederick Cuny. "It is naive to believe that an agency can go into a society and provide a structure which meets their definition of shelter or of a house, without participating in the process through which houses are normally provided", Cuny adds.

What goes for houses also goes for food and other goods. Stories abound in the relief field of completely inappropriate aid: the British charity that sent packs of tea, tissues and Tampax; the European Community sending powdered milk into an earthquake area where few cows had perished, but there was no water; and the West German charity which constructed 1,000 polystyrene igloos which proved too hot to live in. But the igloos could not be dismantled or moved. They had to be burned down, and when burning they gave off toxic fumes. Tins of chicken cooked in pork-fat have been sent to Moslem countries which do not eat pork. Blankets donated to India were donated by India to Nepal, which donated them back to India; the blankets were never needed or used. Turkey after a 1983 earthquake asked donors not to send any medicine or second-hand clothes, but a Northern donor flew in a few days later with a planeload of precisely these items — and a TV crew to cover the distribution.

Tony Jackson of OXFAM has found potato crisps, slimming foods,

A peasant farmer in the Ethiopian Highlands collects butteroil from European Community surpluses during the 1984 drought. This is one of the few forms in which milk products can be of any use to drought victims.

children's sweet fruit drinks and spaghetti sauce sent as food aid to Chad, Guatemala, Kampuchea and the Dominican Republic.

The Red Cross delivered 3,000 tents to the town of San Martín after the 1976 Guatemalan earthquake. Some $850,000 had been donated for this relief effort, and photos appearing in a later Red Cross brochure showed neat rows of tents. But despite efforts by the Guatemalan Army to virtually march the "victims" into the tents at gunpoint, the townsfolk declined; they wanted to be near their possessions and livestock. After two weeks, seven tents were occupied.

A major problem with relief is that the "relief period" following a sudden, violent disaster — as opposed to the reconstruction and rehabilitation periods, which may last some years — is very short; some experts put it at only 48 hours. Depending on climate, if victims have not found shelter, warmth, water and at least the hope of food within a day or two, it is too late. Few international relief agencies can deliver in such a short time. Such necessities are almost always more quickly available near the disaster area. So when tents and blankets arrive from Europe, the victims are either sheltered and warm, or past help.

Yet human nature dictates that when a plane lands with free goods, people will stop what they are doing and queue for hours to get whatever is available, whether they need it or not. Thus relief can actually slow down reconstruction and interfere with self-help.

Examples of inappropriate aid raise the question of to whom the agencies and other "intervenors" are accountable. Who forms their constituency? Ian Davis, from Oxford Polytechnic, UK, looked at the accountability of various outsiders: UN agencies, overseas governments, overseas charities, foreign experts and local elite. He found that none is accountable to the victims of the quake, except in the cases of overseas charities and local elite when they work through grassroots groups, as when the Red Cross works through the local Red Cross chapters or other international volunteer agencies work through local organisations. UN agencies and foreign government agencies are officially accountable to the recipient government and — in the case of national agencies — to their home governments. But in practice, on the disaster scene, they are accountable to no one except a possible journalistic exposé.

In 1976, when fighting had died down in Lebanon, farmers were discouraged from planting crops because of the large amounts of food aid coming in. Two UN agencies — the World Food Programme and UNICEF — were both planning massive import programmes, but were not only not consulting the recipients, they were not consulting one another, according to Cuny, who was working there at the time.

It would be unfair to put all the blame for inappropriate help on foreign agencies. Very often the national governments of the afflicted countries are insensitive, to say the least, to the needs of the victims. Given that human activity causes or exacerbates many natural disasters, then the governments of the victim nations have a large responsibility in doing so little to prevent these disasters. Once a calamity has occurred, government policies often complicate relief work and rehabilitation. In some situations, the needs of afflicted populations are neglected. In others, security problems, real or alleged for political reasons, prevent relief agencies from operating efficiently.

In most disasters, the military plays a key role in restoring order. This follows European and US practices in the 1950s and 1960s, and makes a certain amount of sense because the military can get self-sufficient units to the field quickly, has good communications and access to transport and heavy machinery. It is a disciplined organisation. But the military does things in a military manner. Army units have been known to move into a disaster area like an invading army and to treat the survivors like prisoners of war, ordering them here and there. In some cases troops have organised victims in orderly, compact tent camps — far from their domestic animals and the homes they want to rebuild. The density of such camps can encourage the spread of disease. Such a military approach can create feelings of helplessness and passivity among the victims which would not be there if they were allowed to get on with the job.

"A disaster is a time when people need to get together and develop collective responses. A military hierarchy of decision-making can discourage and inhibit the process", writes Frederick Cuny. It can inhibit the rebuilding process in more concrete ways. After the 1972 Managua earthquake, the remains of buildings were bulldozed to provide a bare, flat landscape for reconstruction. But every two buildings that collapsed could have provided enough building material for one new building — material which was destroyed.

At a workshop on disaster management in Hyderabad, India, in 1980, Lt Col Gurdip Singh said on behalf of the Indian military establishment that in a disaster there was too much reliance on the armed forces by both the national government and the population. He said that dependence on the military (a federal force) removed responsibility from state governments, where it belonged. The discussion which followed revealed mixed feelings about the use of the military, with some observers noting that resources should be maximised in times of a disaster, and that the military was a resource.

The home government can make mistakes without resorting to the military. Between 1966 and 1976, Turkey lost 10,618 people in six major earthquakes. Foreign relief workers have praised both the Turkish Army and the Red Crescent Society with their efficiency in providing relief after quakes; but the government has been widely criticised for its rebuilding and rehabilitation programmes. Over the decade the government response was to send to the disaster areas prefabricated houses built at factories in Ankara. These units, conceived by urban architects in the capital, are difficult to repair and extend, are cold at night and hot in the daytime, provide no winter housing for animals, follow no regional variations in housing types and are often erected on prime agricultural land, safe from landslide but exposed to seasonal winds.

More recently, according to British architect Stuart Lewis, the Turkish government has been phasing out the prefab construction. It now plans to build large apartment blocks in the disaster-prone regions and house victims in those for about a year while their villages are rebuilt, probably by outside labour. This new approach raises questions about the suitability of the new homes and about the wisdom of separating victims from homes, animals and fields for a year.

If the government cannot get it right, can outsiders hope to fare better? A foreign relief agency erected polystyrene igloos after a Turkish earthquake; they blew down.

The relief "constituency"

An examination of the "constituencies" of the foreign intervenors in disasters — whether UN agency, foreign government or relief agency — helps explain the mixed motives.

Rarely, except when intervenors work through local organisations, does this constituency include the actual victims of the disaster. For the big Western governments, the constituency is the voters at home — especially around election time — and the other branches of government, especially those concerned with foreign policy.

Over the period 1965-73, the total of US government disaster aid exceeded that of the rest of the international community in five of the nine years. In the case of some disasters, US aid exceeded that provided by total country self-help, according to British geographer Phil O'Keefe. However, by themselves these figures give the wrong impression. Over that nine-year period, in-country self-help more than doubled the amount of external assistance received. The domestic self-help is also probably underestimated. So despite international relief efforts, the local people still do most of their own "relieving" and reconstructing.

It is possible to make three broad generalisations about disaster aid from the North. First, it is highly variable and follows no logic of need and cost-effectiveness. Second, it tends to follow the pattern of the donor country's development and military aid; i.e., relief aid tends to go to allies and those already getting aid. Third, a lot of "relief" is merely the export of surplus commodities.

As for lack of logic, the most telling statistic is that the dead seem to attract more "relief" than those still struggling. A ranking of disaster types in terms of numbers killed during the 1970s, beginning with the deadliest, would read as follows: earthquake, cyclone, civil strife, drought and flood (see Figure 3). In terms of numbers affected, the ranking is almost reversed: drought (almost 25 million), flood, civil strife, cyclone and earthquake (about two million — see Figure 5). But a ranking of donor response to League of Red Cross and Red Crescent Societies appeals during the 1970s (see Figure 12) reads: civil strife, earthquake, cyclone, flood, drought. So except for the civil strife category, disasters that kill a few quickly get much more "relief" than disasters that grind people down slowly.

Accidents of newsworthiness and politics can affect response. In Europe, the attempt by the Ethiopian government under Haile Selassie to virtually ignore the drought in the early 1970s became an international scandal with enormous media coverage. Contributions through volunteer agencies exceeded $21 million. In the United States, the media was focused on Watergate, and US aid was only about $1.5 million. In early 1984, US congressmen trying to vote through more grain for drought-afflicted African nations were frustrated because the appropriation had been tacked onto a controversial vote for military aid for Central America.

Some disasters are simply more fashionable than others. In 1983, the Red Cross launched separate appeals for Polish food needs and for the Brazilian drought victims. Poland got four times more than was appealed for. By the end of 1983, the northeastern Brazilian drought appeal had brought in only 2.4% of the expressed needs, though this figure rose slowly to above 50% by March 1984. A November 1983 Red Cross appeal for Turkish earthquake victims almost immediately brought in $233 per person assisted; the Brazil drought appeal, also launched in November, had gathered no more than 56 cents per person to be assisted by the end of the year. The League launched a total of 48 international appeals in 1983, the biggest for drought victims in India and Mauritania. But Poland and Turkey got 26.7% of the total gift value of $57 million raised that year; India got one-third of the amount appealed for, and Mauritania got about half.

In Europe, appeals from former colonies in Africa and Asia tend to raise more money than disasters in Latin America. But the United States, which regards Latin America as its sphere of influence, is more disposed to help those governments which it regards as favourably disposed to its policies. During the 1973-74 crop year, the US contributed $130 million dollars to the Sahel region. At the same time the US also airlifted $2.2 billion to Israel, during the October 1973 Yom Kippur War. And in fiscal 1974-75, the US Congress approved $700 million for South Vietnam. Africa, which tends to suffer most from drought and famine today, is low in US aid priorities; less than 10% of USAID foreign appropriation goes to Africa, and the majority of that to only 10 African states.

US "PL 480" food aid, which covers both concessional sales and donations, does go to feed people in need. But it is unreliable; when US farmers can get higher prices abroad for their grain, the PL 480 programme is drastically cut. During the Sahel famine, low domestic cereal prices encouraged the US government to pay $3 billion to US farmers not to produce food. The downturn in production and large Soviet purchases meant there was little US grain available for aid. The United States gave 6.1 million tonnes of wheat in food aid in 1970, but it provided only 2.5 million tonnes in 1973. In the 1974 fiscal year, more than 50% of the Food for Peace shipments went to countries reflecting US security concerns such as Vietnam, Cambodia, Laos, Malta, Jordan and Israel.

Politics — along with a growing sense of pride and a growing realisation of the limitations of foreign relief efforts — also has a role to play in limiting what disaster-stricken nations will accept today. After the Guatemala City earthquake of 1976, Guatemala refused to accept aid from Britain because the two countries were in dispute over Belize. China, India, Mexico and the Philippines are all countries which have recently declined disaster aid in certain cases, apparently through a mixture of pride and seeing no real gain in accepting it.

Charity and its motives

Governments are not the only relief organisations which overlook the needs of disaster victims in planning their activities. The non-governmental relief agencies may also be prone to similar "political" motivation.

Voluntary agencies find relief efforts helpful in book-keeping in two ways. First, delivering a planeload of food to earthquake victims generates great amounts of publicity, and publicity brings in more contributions to the agency. Such efforts catch more press attention than, say, helping villagers build cyclone-resistant houses. This may be one reason relief agencies expend so much effort to be first in getting goods to disaster areas, even if there is no way to distribute the goods to victims once they arrive. Such publicity is a two-edged sword, as it can mean that agencies let the media set priorities for them. OXFAM disaster co-ordinator Marcus Thompson describes how difficult it is to explain to an OXFAM donor why the agency is not involved in a flood which has just been shown on television: "…'Of course it's a disaster; I saw it on the news. Send food in', the donor is likely to tell me. It is hard pressure to ignore."

Second, volunteer agencies and charities like to be able to demonstrate that a high percentage of the funds collected go to "the field", and that only a small percentage stays home for such things as salaries and office rent. Disaster relief efforts are a great help in making this ratio appear impressive to would-be donors, because a disaster relief operation — whether effective or ineffective — may consume a great deal of money and material with relatively little manpower overheads. Other activities which may keep experts in the field for long periods can make this ratio of expenditure look less favourable.

There have also been charges that disaster relief appeals are planned not as a response to disasters but as a response to fund-raising strategies. One or two big campaigns a year (especially around Christmas time) for dramatic events like earthquakes tend to pull in many more donations than a long-term appeal for those affected by drought.

The debate over the motives and efficiency of relief has not been ignored by the charities. The UK charities — the British Red Cross Society, Save the Children Fund, Christian Aid, CAFOD (the Catholic charity) and OXFAM — have all banded together to form the Disasters Emergency Committee (DEC). It pools information and launches joint appeals for funds; each organisation disposes of its share according to its interests. DEC has helped avoid competition between appeals and has raised the amounts the appeals can raise. After the Vietnam war, Save the Children, a UK relief-focused organisation, wanted to launch a DEC appeal for relief. War on Want argued that the disaster was continuing and required a longer term effort. War on Want has since left DEC, dissatisfied with its concentration on relief rather than on continuing development aid. OXFAM is also moving away from "relief" toward development.

Frederick Cuny has been involved directly in relief operations in the Biafra war, the Bangladesh civil war and the Lebanese fighting; he has also participated in relief work in Israel, Burundi, Nicaragua, Honduras, Guatemala and Peru. He believes that:

> "A lot of these (large relief) agencies have known for a long time that their programmes do not work. However, they respond to pressure not only from their own donors but from the countries they are working in. Local governments sometimes don't have any better idea than the agencies of what's going on in the field."

Cuny described a large US voluntary agency as being simply "too big" and "locked into providing free assistance. Their entire advertising campaign is based around giving money for welfare for poor people in developing countries. Because of this policy, they can't sell the food or other materials when it is appropriate. I have heard the director talk about why he has to keep doing this. I guess it is more important to have the money coming in than to worry about where it is going or what it is doing."

Food as relief

There has been such a backlash against food aid recently that organisations such as the World Food Programme (WFP) believe that it soon may become difficult to mount any successful appeals for such aid in emergencies.

In early 1984, FAO Director-General Edouard Saouma asked for 1.6 million tonnes of food aid for the 24 African countries most affected by

Mark Edwards/Earthscan

Peasants in Ethiopia's Wollo Region divide drought relief grain among themselves. Well-organised Peasant Associations are responsible for sharing out the grain, a system which supports rather than interferes with local leadership systems.

drought. Though much of this aid, if raised, will go astray and be used inefficiently, it would be a tragedy if people starved because of changing aid fashions in the North. Any criticism of food aid for disaster relief must be balanced by the knowledge that food aid can and does save lives.

This book is not addressing the complex debate on food aid in general; our discussion centres on the effectiveness of using food as part of post-disaster relief. About 70% of all food aid is given or sold on concessional terms to Third World governments, and most of this is resold to help these governments' budgets. The remaining 30% — "project food aid" — is designated for free distribution to the poor. Only 10% of all food aid is used for disaster relief and feeding refugees.

OXFAM's Tony Jackson, whose book *Against the Grain* (Oxford, 1982) best describes the problems connected with various types of food aid, says firmly in his conclusions: "Food aid is often needed for emergency relief and this will often entail imports, especially for refugees". He asserts elsewhere: "A well-organised and equitable relief programme is possible". He gives as an example of such a programme the efforts following the destruction in southwest Dominican Republic by Hurricanes David and Frederick in 1979. The Netherlands office of the international relief agency

Caritas organised the import of food, paid for by the Dutch, first from nearby Caribbean islands and then from the Netherlands itself. WFP brought in food from Haiti. Some 300,000 people received food over a five-month period. The distribution programme was designed and run locally, and recipients were told they would get food for five months only, so reliance on food aid was not institutionalised.

But there are many cases in which food aid programmes after disasters have done more harm than good, over both the short and the long term.

In 1972, drought in New Guinea was accompanied by 30 nights of ground frost over a four-month period. Colonial administrators, who had not experienced such frosts before, declared a "disaster" and organised the import of Australian rice and Japanese tinned fish to feed 150,000 people over an 18-month period. Canadian geographer Eric Waddell, describing the New Guinea effort, comments sardonically that "as a relief operation it was a total success. No one died, and the nutritional status of the population actually increased..." In fact, the native population, which had been dealing with drought and frosts for centuries, had its own elaborate and effective traditional methods of coping with them, including migrating and being "hosted" by unaffected populations. But the New Guinea people were never consulted by the colonial administrators during this particular drought. The result of the relief effort was that the old coping systems broke down; customary hosts became unwilling to receive frost victims, passing responsibility to government and relief organisations. People acquired a taste for imported food and for more protein, and became less self-sufficient.

"There were signs of local and regional autonomy being undermined and institutional dependence encouraged as a result of the venture", Waddell says. The people could cope with frosts, but not with disaster experts or the government.

Jackson offers many other examples of food aid gone wrong. Much of it, he says, is wholly unnecessary. The Guatemalan earthquake, which did not affect crops, coincided with a huge harvest. So much food was sent that "we knocked the bottom out of the grain market in the country for nine to 12 months", said the *New York Times*. US anthropologist George Morren Jr claims this aid "did more economic damage to farmers than the earthquake itself".

Food aid often arrives much too late. Food relief for a 1977 drought in Haiti arrived in 1978, during a good harvest. Though no longer needed, it was distributed because, in the words of a UN official, it was "not economically feasible" to return it. Grenada asked for European Community skimmed milk powder after flooding in 1976. It arrived in 1979, in time for another emergency.

Once begun, food aid may never stop. Since the 1976 earthquake, Guatemala has continued to receive much larger amounts of non-disaster food aid than it received before. Haiti first received food aid after Hurricane

Hazel in 1954; according to one priest, "it never stopped coming".

Post-disaster food aid is often of the wrong type. Some examples of this are listed above. During the Biafran war of 1968, Switzerland sent large amounts of Emmenthaler cheese to people who normally drank little milk and had never eaten cheese. Relief workers had to bury the cheese.

But the problems go beyond the waste of time and money. An OXFAM-World Neighbours official noted that "totally dishonest" local leaders began to emerge after the Guatemala quake, looked up to because they had a knack for fraudulently getting more free food from competing relief agencies. "With larger and larger quantities of free food coming in, there are increased incentives to corruption.... Groups that had worked together previously became enemies over the question of recipients of free food." A report from the voluntary agency Caritas' office in Haiti following the 1977 drought said, "At last we hope to rid ourselves of the yoke of imported food, which has no other effect than of diminishing community spirit, while encouraging passivity in people".

There is a large body of opinion which holds that relief food aid has actually been responsible for much of the turmoil Bangladesh has suffered since the 1971 civil war. So much food aid poured in after the fighting that market prices for rice fell. Farmers planted less; production fell, and as production fell, agencies sent in more food. In 1975, World Food Programme director Trevor Page asked donor countries to stop sending food. He told a meeting that the more food which came in, the more starvation there appeared to be. By the mid-1970s, the ports were becoming jammed by food shipments, and Bengali farmers began to sell their food to marketeers who smuggled it into India, where they could make a bigger profit. By the start of the 1980s, the aid and relief agencies had accomplished little more than to build up "a dependency relationship on foreign resources", according to US disaster consultant Frederick Cuny. "Now the idea of having a foreign adviser has permeated the entire Bengali society, all the way down to the village level, to the point where nobody makes decisions unless it's been OK'd by a foreigner, and the foreigners are much less equipped than the Bengalis to run Bangladesh."

The controversy over food aid generally and disaster relief food aid in particular has not been ignored by the WFP, which noted in a 1982 issue of *World Food Programme News* that wherever possible WFP purchases its emergency and relief assistance food regionally, as for instance when purchasing for such countries as Burma, Thailand and Zimbabwe. It is able to bring food aid to disaster areas in sufficient quantities and in time to prevent starvation by diverting food from development projects in a given country or even from ships at sea. While asserting that a substantial part of its relief resources was used to feed starving people too weak to work after disaster had struck, WFP advocated the phasing out of free relief distribution as soon as local governments could organise constructive rehabilitation.

Tom Learmonth/Earthscan

Queuing for food relief organised by a Bangladesh youth group after the 1980 floods in Dhaka. Long waits for foreign relief can slow down the recovery process.

The radicals

There are a growing number of disaster experts, dubbed "radicals" by many of their technology-oriented colleagues, who strongly question the traditional work of the relief agencies.

The radicals say that it is the people living on the margins in both city and countryside who are both most prone and most vulnerable to disasters. They see the numbers of these "marginalised" people growing, both because of increasing populations and because of a world economic order which steadily increases the gap between the North and the South.

"Concentrating the urban proletariat in 'favelas' (shantytowns) and obliging the rural peasantry to develop cash crop production for export are but two illustrations of this process which intensifies disaster proneness", writes Canadian geographer Eric Waddell. Population growth — fuelled by the poor's search for security by having more children — is seen more as a symptom than as a cause of increasing marginalisation.

These experts say they are tired of the habit of "blaming the victim: for example, shifting cultivators causing erosion and landslips, overgrazing by pastoralists promoting desertification, suburbanites choosing to live in floodplains, high fertility in the Third World, and so on", writes US agriculturalist George Morren Jr. "Such stereotyped examples do possess the grain of truth necessary in scientific circles. A broader view would see these as frequently involving responses of ordinary people to development acts over which they had no control: the commercialisation and expansion of agriculture, urbanisation, demand for labour and the like."

The relief agencies are seen by the radicals as the agents not of the victims but of wealthy Northern governments. Their prime concern is to return disaster victims to "the status quo". Yet it is precisely that status quo which makes them vulnerable. So by maintaining the status quo, the radicals argue, the agencies ensure that disasters will continue to increase in the Third World. And disaster mitigation work relying on high technology merely reinforces the conditions of underdevelopment and increases marginalisation.

"Since it is the institutional and structural order which is at fault, disaster research and relief should formulate models and strategies which challenge this order", writes Waddell. "These should be based on the preservation and reinforcement of indigenous responses and involve a minimum of internal intervention (national or international)."

...and "the Reds"

Many disaster experts disagree strongly with such views; others find such arguments too theoretical to be of any use. "All that is very well", commented one architect concerned with housing and disasters, "but it is still important after a quake to get roofs on houses in such a way that they will stay there."

Most Red Cross societies traditionally take a conservative and cautious view on the nature of their intervention in disasters. The reasons for this are understandable, most stemming from the very origins of the movement. The Red Cross has always been an emergency organisation. It was born on the battlefield, and it comes into its own in times of conflict. To be effective in its unique protection of prisoners of war and aid to the wounded, it feels it must be seen to be neutral. Its leaders feel that if it were to start championing social causes, it might get involved in politics, and lose its neutral image.

Yet many Red Cross societies have been gradually changing their policies, and working more and more through local Red Cross societies in disaster-stricken countries. Flying goods halfway around the world is becoming the exception more than the rule. Most purchases are being made in the affected area or nearby, after close cooperation with local Red Cross representatives.

There are 132 national Red Cross and Red Crescent Societies, with over 210 million members, and these represent a broad range of opinion. The Swedish Red Cross is shifting away from what it calls the traditional approach of "giving emergency assistance in isolated disaster events". It is developing a policy of setting aside 20-30% of all emergency funds for longer-term preventive actions. It is already getting involved in community-based rural programmes together with sister societies in a few Third World countries. Similar policies are emerging within the other Nordic Red Cross societies.

The disaster processes involved in drought and famine can only be met by a development process, aimed at prevention of causes, the Swedish Red Cross believes. Disaster assistance must go hand in hand with development assistance and is futile on a short-term basis. And the development process must be one that improves the conditions of both the natural environment and many millions of poor people. Such work may appear to involve political activity not in keeping with the Red Cross position of neutrality. However, as former OXFAM director Brian Walker pointed out at a 1984 Swedish Red Cross symposium on the prevention of disasters, the decision not to get involved in development activity is just as "political" as a decision to get involved. Neither position is "neutral".

The entire Red Cross movement seems to be gradually coming around to this way of thinking. The League of Red Cross and Red Crescent Societies has teamed up with the World Health Organization and UNICEF to prevent and treat child-killing diseases in developing nations. At the Red Cross General Assembly meeting in 1983 it was agreed that, in addition to its emergency role, the Red Cross must recognise its responsibilities to work "towards the reduction of the impact of famine and towards ultimate prevention". In line with this decision, Red Cross societies in West Africa were designing programmes to help combat desertification.

If the Red Cross starts to speak out loudly against the alarming disaster trends, and changes its way of approaching disaster problems, it could have a very important impact on public opinion.

Chapter 8

Disasters and development

The preceding chapters indicate that many millions of poor people in Third World countries are more or less permanently affected by disaster processes and that hundreds of millions are vulnerable to floods and droughts, and to shortages of food, water and fuelwood. As natural disasters and many resource shortages are on the increase, it is obvious that current development efforts are having too little effect in these areas. This may be partly because rural development is rarely the priority it ought to be.

But the previous discussion also suggests that the prevention of many Third World disasters *is* possible, necessary and urgent. It *should* be possible, since the causes and effects of disasters depend to such a large degree on human activities. As it is possible, it is also necessary; the unnecessary harm to people and to the environment has reached enormous proportions, and emergency relief cannot adequately meet the needs of the victims.

Prevention is urgent, as the increasing frequency and severity of disasters are nearing the point of being unmanagable. In large parts of Asia, Africa and Latin America, the ecological base for human existence is being so damaged that it can no longer support the growing populations of these regions.

Most disaster problems in the Third World are unsolved development problems. Disaster prevention and mitigation is thus primarily an aspect of development. In some regions, disaster prevention should be the major goal of development assistance from Northern countries. Also, relief interventions should be linked, where possible, with development programmes. Disasters can actually become "vehicles for change" and involve both development and relief agencies in long-term programmes aimed both at development and at disaster prevention and mitigation.

"Disasters are not unforeseen events, and the technology now exists to identify the hazards that threaten a community and to estimate the areas and the settlements that will be affected", argues US disaster consultant Frederick Cuny.

"In most places and segments of society where calamities are occurring, the natural events are about as certain as anything within a person's lifetime'', writes Canadian geographer Kenneth Hewitt. "Should a sane social order disregard the likelihood of massive destruction, simply because it is not quite sure on which day of which year in the next decade or two it will occur?... Are people unaware and poorly prepared because natural extremes are rare and unpredictable? Are they indifferent to the possibility of flood or earthquake because preoccupied with 'present gratifications'? Or is it because the everyday conditions of work, life support, social and mental security or the artificial environment require all of their risk-avoiding and risk-taking energies?''

"The very essence of disaster mitigation is long-term planning'', says Marcus Thompson, OXFAM's disaster co-ordinator. "The very essence of Third World poverty is the struggle of day-to-day existence.''

When Ian Davis of Oxford Polytechnic, UK, and fellow researchers visited northern Pakistan near its borders with Afghanistan and China, they found people living with the threat of rockslides on one side of their houses and erosion and flooding on the other. The whole area was subject to earthquakes and water supply problems. They found few examples of families adapting their homes and living patterns to these risks. Asked why this was so, the people said that they had far greater worries than natural disasters. One householder was amazed that so many experts should come so far about such a trivial matter.

The local people were more concerned with their children's education or lack of it, their health and the scarcity of medicine in the dispensaries, and the difficulties of selling their crops at a decent price, which relates to the problems of access to markets in this inaccessible terrain.

"So vulnerability to natural hazards has to be recognised within the cultural and economic context of poverty and deprivation. And as with our own society, long-term logical action is frequently overwhelmed by short-term expediency'', Davis wrote. Yet the group of experts did identify realistic ways in which the people's natural disaster risks could be reduced.

Those who would intervene efficiently and helpfully in the social events which are natural disasters — whether the intervenors come from inside or outside the afflicted nation — they intervene in the society of the victims. Most of these societies are poor.

Over the years, certain guidelines have been formulated by organisations — especially non-governmental organisations — which intervene in poor Third World societies. The majority of these organisations are concerned not with natural disasters but with a vague concept called "development''. There is even less agreement on what is meant by "development'' than on what is meant by "disaster''; and there is also considerable dispute on how much good is done by these "development intervenors''. But development-oriented groups have found ways of at least avoiding the certainty of failure. These include such steps as:

* Rigorously defining the goals of the intervention. Increasing the output of the subsistence farmer will require very different programmes than increasing the agricultural output of a nation.
* Defining the target group. One does not help smallholders by providing wealthy landowners with tubewells.
* Carefully studying the target group to see how it operates already. The protein intake of a society which does not for religious reasons eat pork is not going to be improved by a pig farming project.
* Talking to the target group to see if it shares the same perception of the problem. Those who do not see a connection between poor sanitation and disease are unlikely to take the trouble to use latrines, freely supplied or otherwise.
* Working with groups and individuals already respected in the society, and remaining answerable to those groups and individuals as the work progresses, as changes and adjustments are needed.

These guidelines appear obvious. Yet the classic fly-in relief operation breaks many of these "rules", and thus will often do more harm than good. As discussions of post-disaster food and shelter relief have shown, such efforts can actually set back development.

"Relief and reconstruction programmes cannot be regarded or conducted as separate or distinct operations. They must be conducted in the same manner as normal development programmes", wrote Frederick Cuny. "Organisations which fail to recognise this can set back or even wipe out years of progress toward social and economic development."

Field staff training workshops involving Save the Children, OXFAM and World Vision in 1982 arrived at the same basic conclusion: "While 'disasters' require urgent relief intervention, the issues involved in giving aid are the same as in any development situation. Normal development priorities, policies and, as far as possible, normal procedures should be adopted in disaster situations." These meetings also recommended that field staff should be the key element in deciding whether and how an agency should respond, and "field staff recommendations should not be outweighed by domestic pressures for agency action arising from media coverage of the disaster". Also, agencies "should minimise dependence on expatriate relief workers".

But is it realistic to suggest that these development intervention rules can be followed and that a "development aspect" can be injected into a relief effort in the midst of or just following a major disaster, when all is chaos and the objective is saving lives and "getting things back to normal"?

During and after the Bangladesh civil war in 1971 there were thousands of apparently helpless people crowded into refugee camps, and the large relief agencies were pouring in food aid. Workers of the Mennonite Central Committee (a foreign relief agency) in these camps decided to minimise food imports. Instead, they encouraged people to convert all possible land to growing food; they cut two-way roads down the middle and planted half in crops; they made people walk single file on pathways and used half the paths for foodcrops. Thus the camps in which the Mennonites were working produced much of their own food.

The vast experience which innovative agencies have collected over years of coping with disasters have thrown up ways of turning most relief operations into an opportunity for furthering development. "We rarely find any reason for departing from 'development rules' in disasters", said Thompson of OXFAM. "In development work, you don't give away food without having thought carefully about motives, needs and timing; the same holds for disasters. There are exceptions: you may occasionally hand out clothes after a flood, when people were literally left standing in what they had on when disaster struck. You rarely hand out clothes in development work."

Yet in 1983 when civil strife in Assam left many people burnt out of their homes, OXFAM did not give them clothes. Instead, working through a local organisation, it helped them to get new looms. "This allowed them to make the sort of clothes they wanted. There is a local tradition of looms in every house, so it fitted neatly with what they did already. It gave them a means of making a little money. And we were able to make a few minor improvements in the local loom at the same time", said Thompson.

Disaster: a spur for development?

Disasters have a creative side. They can spur a society toward radical — sometimes even beneficial — change.

The 1972 Nicaraguan earthquake which flattened half of Managua, and the government's handling of relief and rehabilitation, concentrated resentment against the corrupt Somoza regime, which fell in 1979. Over 15,000 people died in the Tabas earthquake of northern Iran in 1978. The national Red Lion and Sun Society (the Iranian equivalent of the Red Cross — now the Red Crescent Society) handed out blankets and tents, but the fundamentalist religious leaders organised relief which criticised the government. This was part of the process toward the fall of the Shah in 1979. Attempts by the regime of Ethiopian Emperor Haile Selassie to virtually hush up the 1973-74 drought there — and charges of misappropriation of relief food once it arrived — hastened his downfall in 1974. The 1970 East Bangladesh cyclone emphasised the difference in resources between East and West Pakistan, and helped to spur the political events which led to the civil war which created Bangladesh the next year.

Disaster has also encouraged social change in the North. The London Building Acts were motivated by the fire which destroyed London in 1666, according to Ian Davis. London's Thames Embankment of the 19th century contains a major sewer and eliminates the previous dumping of raw sewage into the river. Reformers were able to push it through following cholera outbreaks. Flooding on Canvey Island near London killed 300 people in 1953; this disaster helped clear the way for the multi-million dollar Thames flood barrier.

"Disasters often precipitate major changes in both the economic and political life of a country", Cuny wrote. When an earthquake demolishes housing, it not only creates the need for new housing — a need which agencies can take advantage of to improve housing — but it graphically demonstrates the shortcomings of traditional housing.

Why wait?

Discussions of housing relief lead to the question of why agencies need to wait for a disaster to help "disaster victims". Consequently some agencies, the Red Cross among them, have started to stockpile building materials, food, medicines and other emergency goods close to regions which are prone to disasters. But such plans raise the question of why, if an agency can get materials near a "pre-disaster" site, it must withhold them until after the disaster —especially if their use could make houses safer and save lives when the disaster strikes. (Part of the answer is that disasters provide both a need for and a motive to use the new materials.)

But why do many agencies concerned with disasters tend to wait for a disaster before acting? Organisations concerned with health are moving more and more toward disease prevention — rather than withholding action until presented with illness. Groups concerned with peace have never considered waiting for war to act. In Western societies, a fire chief does not sit in his fire station waiting for fires. He works on fire prevention.

If relief agencies can concern themselves with "pre-disaster strategies", why cannot they concern themselves with the "pre-disaster victims"? Many development and volunteer agencies are already doing this, and as noted at the end of the previous chapter, the Red Cross is moving in this direction.

The pre-disaster victims are easy to identify. They live in disaster-prone areas in conditions of poor housing and poor nutrition which make them more vulnerable to disasters. It is the poor who are most vulnerable and among these poor it is the children, the aged, the widowed, the handicapped and the malnourished who are especially at risk.

Helping the "pre-disaster victims"

Theories on ways to minimise the effects of disasters have been buffeted by fashion. The Cold War of the 1950s led to stress on "preparedness". During the highly technological 1960s, the emphasis switched to "prevention", and

Mark Edwards/Earthscan

Rows of trees planted across millet fields in southern Niger have decreased wind erosion and increased yields. Villagers divide the proceeds of wood sales when the rows are thinned.

then during the 1970s, "mitigation" came into fashion. Now it appears that a more sophisticated form of preparedness may be the strategy of the 1980s.

Preparedness has to do with having everything and everybody in place before a disaster so that order can more quickly be established during the chaos that the event will bring. Examples include stockpiles and action plans. Prevention involves such things as building levees to prevent flooding, and seeding to dissipate cyclones. It is very expensive and, in the case of rivers which are rapidly silting, must be done repeatedly. Mitigation has to do with pre-disaster measures to minimise effects: zoning and building laws to cope with earthquakes and cyclones; drought-resistant crops; public education and insurance.

Few non-government agencies concerned with disasters can afford to get involved in expensive, traditional prevention activities such as building levees. Nor can agencies, except perhaps the large UN bodies, expect to get involved in the "top-down" national preparedness and mitigation strategies. But there are numerous opportunities for working with the potential victims to make their environment less prone and themselves less vulnerable. Such programmes would have several things in common, all being:

* directed toward those on the margins;
* family-based and village-based;

* environmentally sustainable;
* concerned with protection and rehabilitation of soil, water and forests;
* aimed at reducing poverty among the vulnerable;
* concerned with nutrition, as it is the malnourished who are the most vulnerable to the hardships accompanying disaster, especially those interrupting food supplies;
* concerned with fostering self-reliance, as this is the only way the programmes themselves will be sustainable;
* focused on subsistence agriculture, as it is the peasant farmers whose lives and livelihoods are most vulnerable to most disasters.

Agencies which could work these goals into their programmes would be making people less vulnerable to disaster and less in need of "relief and rehabilitation" after disasters. They would also be improving the overall quality of people's lives, not just the quality of their lives during a cyclone or earthquake. A subsistence farmer able to cope with a drought is better able to cope in non-drought years.

There is a danger in the realisation that disaster vulnerability and poverty are inseparable. It can lead one up the classic cul-de-sac: the Catch 22 of all development, and the rationalisation of many Northern opponents of development assistance. Their argument is: "The poor are vulnerable. Poverty cannot be eliminated. Therefore, nothing can be done".

In fact, there are many low-cost projects which can both mitigate the effects of disaster and help to "develop" a Third World community. Some disaster experts are fond of saying that almost any good development project will alleviate the effects of a disaster. Cuny points out that the introduction of high-yielding wheat varieties into India in the 1960s-70s not only improved the nation's nutritional balance but helped reduce the possibility of a major famine due to the failure of the rice crop. Also, savings and loan programmes introduced into Guatemala by the cooperative movement mitigated the economic effects of disasters and gave people money reserves with which to rebuild after the 1976 earthquake.

Natural disasters are failures in interactions between vulnerable people and a vulnerable environment. Disaster mitigation, therefore, should aim at changes to improve both human and environmental conditions and the interactions between them. One cannot be isolated from the other. The major disaster problems are essentially unsolved development problems.

The following are a few examples of low-cost development-type programmes suitable for organisations concerned about disasters.

Drought

Droughts are never completely rainless. Farmers can cope better with a drought if they can better use what water there is and can be ready to take

Mark Edwards/Earthscan

Hillside terracing holds scarce rainwater in the Ethiopian highlands. The nation's Peasants Associations constructed 700,000 kilometres (453,000 miles) of such terraces from 1977 to 1984 in some of the world's largest Food for Work projects.

advantage of more plentiful rainfall when it comes. And such skills are beneficial to farmers in arid or semi-arid regions, drought or no drought.

Many volunteer agencies are leaving to governments the provision of outright food aid for drought victims. Instead, they are providing seeds and helping with the establishment of very simple seed banks. This is of immediate benefit, because many drought victims will have eaten their seeds and have nothing to plant. It is also of long-term benefit, in that the agencies can — usually at very little cost — supply seeds of more drought-resistant varieties and farmers can get into the habit of drawing from a seed bank. These banks can, by offering a choice of varieties, give farmers the flexibility so necessary in coping with climatic variation.

British agricultural consultant David Morgan notes in a study of the southern African drought which started in 1983: "Many defensive measures which are already available are not implemented. Among the most important of these is the availability of drought-resistant fodder crops". Successful trials have been made of many of the acacia species (thorn-tree) and Mopani *(Colophospermum mopane)* in Southern Africa: cows in Namibia actually gained weight on a diet of edible acacia leaves and twigs mixed with molasses and urea. Grain sorghum, which feeds people in the Sahel, can be a good

Irrigation combats drought at Nakfa, Eritrea. Development efforts continue in the region, despite persistant drought and over two decades of armed struggle.

drought-resistant cattle food in areas of Southern Africa where it is not grown, Morgan writes.

Other important drought-prevention schemes include terracing, reforestation and sand dune stabilisation — techniques aimed at protection against erosion. Most of these techniques are well-known but are not being implemented on a scale large enough to cope with the problems. Here governments and development authorities, as well as agencies presently preoccupied with relief could join together in efforts to multiply existing soil protection programmes.

Water, wind and sand

Rain runs quickly off drought-hardened soils, doing seeds or plants little good and often carrying them along with it. There are a number of very cheap ways to slow this water.

US Peace Corps worker Bill Hereford joined OXFAM's field staff in Burkina-Faso (formerly called Upper Volta) after studying the "micro-catchment" systems which grow trees in the Israeli section of the Negev

Villagers have planted trees across these moving dunes in the Majia Valley, Niger, in the hope of keeping the dunes out of the fertile river valley (foreground). Much of the best Third World disaster mitigation work, like this effort organised by the US volunteer agency CARE, is carried out at the village level by non-governmental organisations.

Desert. As the name suggests, these are very small catchment areas designed to concentrate available water into an even smaller area where a few plants, perhaps even one tree, are planted. On flat ground, rectangular parcels are surrounded by low embankments 10-25 cm (4-10 ins) high, perhaps 10-30 metres (33-98 feet) long. Inside each the ground is made to slope gradually to a smaller basin in which one or a few trees are planted. On slopes, the embankments — made from earth, stones or even millet stalks — may be crescent shaped, along the contour, to focus the water on basins.

OXFAM has taught the people to use a simple surveying tool to find contour lines. A length of plastic pipe is filled with water and laid along the ground with both ends elevated. When the water level at each end is the same, the pipe is lying along a contour line.

Forester Arlene Blade encouraged the people to plant trees which produced cattle fodder, edible fruit or nuts and were good for the soil. But then Blade asked the women for advice on which trees were good for firewood, and found that she had missed several valued species — more often shrubs than trees — which produced excellent fuelwood, grew quickly on degraded ground and were not liked by animals, so did not need constant protection. The farmers, seeing how well the trees grew, quickly adopted the catchment system themselves, without advice, to grow rice, maize, sorghum, millet and groundnuts; and word has been slowly spreading from village to village both by formal demonstration and by word of mouth. By July 1982, some 30 villages had adopted the practice.

Another simple way to make rainwater more useful is to build low rock walls across dry watercourses, so that when the rains come some of the water is stopped long enough to seep into the ground and raise the water table.

Recently researcher Frank Anderson of the International Livestock Centre for Africa (ILCA) in Addis Ababa, Ethiopia, found in an Australian farmyard an ancient horsedrawn iron scoop, of the sort used to dig ponds in 19th century Australia and the United States. It has been redesigned so it can be pulled by two light African zebu cattle and used to build a 3,000 cubic metre (106,000 cu ft) pond in a month. The scoop, which costs $150 to make of sheet metal, offers no training, maintenance or repair problems, and can be used to build ponds, dams, irrigation canals and drainage works. It could bring land previously prone to flooding into cultivation or help provide irrigation for a second, dry-season crop.

Several agencies, including the Salvation Army, are helping local people "harvest" water in the dry Turkana area of northwest Kenya. The rainfall is directed into channels running off the hillsides, the flow stopped by stone dams and run into prepared areas where it seeps into the soil so that crops can be grown.

Planting trees and "live fences" of shrubs can decrease the wind erosion which takes topsoil out of fields and leaves the heavier sand grains behind. CARE, a US voluntary agency, has organised the planting of 20 km (12 miles) of windbreaks per year in Niger's Majia Valley at low cost. Recently the local organisation of villagers has been debating how to divide the proceeds from the first sale of wood as the trees are thinned. Other such windbreak schemes, which can increase grain harvests by 15-25%, are being undertaken in other Sahelian states by volunteer organisations, many of which are also working in dune stabilisation programmes.

Early warning

As discussed in Chapter Two, famine is not simply a lack of food. Even harvest shortfalls of only a few per cent can help precipitate a massive famine.

Satellite photos have not been much help as an early warning system. They also raise all the problems about paying for the photos, getting them interpreted, getting the interpretations to the right people and then taking the appropriate action. Most experts regard government crop statistics — often based on small samples, badly interpreted and "adjusted" to match political needs — as highly unreliable. Thus FAO's Global Information and Early Warning System is often criticised for relying too heavily on government statistics.

Dr John Rivers of London's International Disasters Institute, and other experts, have put forward a low-cost, alternative "early warning system" for crops. They note that, even in farming systems almost entirely based on subsistence rather than cash crops, a tremendous amount of buying and selling (or bartering) goes on in village markets. Prices in such markets reflect the reality of the crops — whether farmers are gearing for scarcity and withholding crops, or sense a bumper harvest and are trying to get rid of grain. "The price graphs normally show smooth dry and wet season curves; but at the first signs of a drought/famine — months before governments or international agencies are aware of a problem — the graphs look as if they were being drawn by someone with a very shaky hand", says Rivers.

In a region like the Sahel, there are enough representatives of voluntary and other agencies in the field to collect price data regularly: simply by buying grain in local markets, and sending the information to a central, small computer. (The political acceptability of this to host governments remains open to question.) John Seasons, nutritional expert at Save the Children Fund, claims that his organisation has through these techniques already successfully "predicted" — or at least been aware of the very early stages of — food shortages.

Floods

Much of the disaster mitigation work associated with floods involves housing, especially in the many big-city shantytowns which are built in flood-prone areas. This work, as in housing programmes in earthquake regions, involves both making the houses disaster-resistant and building better houses after the disaster.

But the Action for Food Production (AFPRO) group of India is taking a much more positive approach to floods in a 500 hectare (1,240 acre) "Living with Floods" experiment in northeastern India along the Goghara Nala River.

"Every year we talk of unprecedented drought and unprecedented floods but forget that this is all due to the unprecedented arrogance of Man who always talks of managing nature and never of living with nature", said AFPRO head Col B.L. Verma. "Man always talks of management of floods and refuses to admit that in India it is floods that manage Man, in spite of the phenomenal advancement in science and technology and astronomical expenditure on flood control."

The AFPRO project villages, lying in a bend in the river and flooded almost yearly, were topographically surveyed. Based on this data, the fields were contoured and drains were dug, all connecting eventually with the river. People living in drainage areas were persuaded to move. The object of the drains is to get flood water out of the fields much more quickly; the villagers are organised to quickly plant a post-monsoon winter crop in October as soon as the water recedes. This can be harvested in March, in time to plant a summer crop irrigated by shallow tubewells worked with mobile pumps owned by the community.

Should the experiment succeed, Verma hopes to extend it to 160,000 hectares (395,000 acres) "and bring hope to the farmer of an increased agricultural production through living with floods". There is scope for such projects on floodplains throughout the Third World.

Cyclones

Much of the development work focused on mitigating cyclone damage centres on housing, especially building more wind-resistant structures, perhaps elevated above the likely storm surge level.

There are other possibilities. One is to plant crops which are less vulnerable to cyclone and storm surge damage, especially on islands where one or two crops dominate. Or crop cycles can be adjusted slightly so that crops are harvested before the beginning of the cyclone season.

Few Third World peasants take out insurance. But cooperatives can allow many to benefit from insurance schemes. Cuny offers the example of the Caribbean island nation of Dominica, where 60% of the farmers produce either bananas or coconuts, mostly on small plots. All farmers belong to a cooperative and sell their crop through the cooperative to one authorised buyer — the Windward Islands Banana Company (WINDBAN) in the case of bananas. WINDBAN was insured before Hurricane David in 1979, and received a settlement of several million dollars. This they divided among farmers on the basis of amount of land cultivated. The farmers got only a little less than they would have received for the sale of their crop. They were thus able to clear, replant and rebuild quickly, which was also in WINDBAN's interests. As they spent their money in the local economy, they helped the recovery of the whole island.

L.D. Pryor, author of *Ecological Mismanagement in Natural Disasters,* maintains that by choosing carefully which species of trees to plant and where to plant them, trees can mitigate the effects of a cyclone by intercepting flying debris. He notes that trees played this role when Cyclone Tracy struck Darwin, Australia, in 1974. Obviously, easily uprooted trees in the wrong places could become hazards themselves.

Earthquakes

Grassroots earthquake-mitigation usually centres around the construction and location of dwellings. Such work improves overall development, and development improvements will mitigate future disasters.

Development agencies have found that the best way to house populations is not to build houses; too few houses get built for money spent. Instead, more houses are built by giving people the means to build their own. The same lessons apply after disasters.

OXFAM, World Neighbours and Frederick Cuny's firm Intertect launched a highly-praised rehousing project after the 1976 Guatemala earthquake. They neither built houses nor gave people money or supplies with which to build. Instead, they provided key materials such as corrugated iron roof sheeting at subsidised prices people could afford. This roofing itself provided shelter until new homes could be built, and the money coming in was used to buy and sell more roofing material than could have been supplied in a straight give-away programme. They trained local builders, built demonstration houses, and gave advice on how to choose safe building sites, even on hillsides, and on how to make heavy adobe blocks safer by setting them in a timber frame. They worked through local cooperatives which the survivors trusted.

For the poorest families who could not afford to pay local builders, they set up mutual aid groups of about five families to build one another's houses. They allowed families to work to pay for the building materials. Though the agencies modified the houses in important ways, they kept the same basic design and used the same building materials, which the people were familiar with.

All of this was possible partly because the programme operated when people needed new houses, when the damage of the earthquake was still very visible and when the survivors could see that old ways were not necessarily good ways.

Cuny has suggested, however, that even the subsidised supply of roofing — an occupation of about nine agencies at the time — may have been unnecessary. "What would have happened if the government, or other organisations, had made a policy decision to underwrite low interest loans through existing loan institutions for everyone in the disaster-affected area, and to develop a government surplus of building materials?" As most people had money to purchase building materials, and as a surplus would have brought prices down, people could have bought their roofing without having to go through a subsidy programme set up by an outside agency.

The Guatemalan rehousing programme was abandoned after staff members received anonymous threats against their lives. "Organising the poor for collective action, even to rebuild their own houses, was an activity viewed with concern by many who wanted no change in the status quo", wrote Cuny.

The Salvation Army and OXFAM launched the "Appropriate

Reconstruction Training and Information Centre" (ARTIC) following the 1977 cyclone and storm surge in Andhra Pradesh, India. Traditional building materials were provided; and Australian architect Mark Windass, working for the Salvation Army, suggested simple ways of making traditional houses safer in cyclones. One of his main findings was that the traditional designs, based on a 2,000-year-old Hindu building code, were well adapted to resist wind. Windass suggested three basic modifications, which increased the cost of each house by only about 5%: treating the posts against wet rot and termites and anchoring them more firmly in the ground; strapping down the beams nailed to these posts; and adding cross-bracing between the bamboo posts. ARTIC used booklets, film shows and even a travelling group of actors, singing and acting out a story about cyclone-resistant houses, to spread the word. Though these improvements make the houses better able to stand up to earthquakes, they also make houses better able to stand up to everyday wear and tear.

Volcano and tsunami disaster mitigation schemes may also be housing-based, but in these two events there will be much more emphasis on the safe siting of settlements and early warning systems. Volunteer agencies may not be able to get directly involved in early warning systems, but can help set up schemes to get these warnings to the poor who lack access to modern communications systems.

The future

Relief agencies are becoming increasingly aware of the need to move away from relief after the disaster, towards disaster prevention, closely integrated with development, so as to reduce vulnerability, especially among the poor.

The Swedish Red Cross is developing a policy to set aside 20-30% of its emergency funds for longer-term preventive actions and is involved in community-based rural programmes together with the national Red Cross societies in a few Third World countries. Other Nordic Red Cross societies are developing similar policies. In June 1984, representatives of UN and non-governmental development and environment organisations met in Stockholm at a symposium sponsored by the Swedish Red Cross, and debated for two days the basic premise that relief agencies can more effectively mitigate the effects of disasters by engaging in sustainable development. After the debate, the participants issued a statement urging the Swedish Red Cross to advocate these ideas "throughout the League of Red Cross and Red Crescent Societies, with a view to securing policy decisions by the League in favour of linking disaster relief to developmental and environmental strategies and, furthermore, in stimulating public opinion, in both donor and recipient countries, in these matters. We further urge the Red Cross and Red Crescent

Societies to cooperate with other developmental and environmental agencies in pursuit of these objectives."

It may be some time before the Red Cross and Red Crescent Societies ascertain the best ways of responding to such urgings. Effective grassroots development activity is perhaps even more complex than effective relief operations. The Red Cross and Red Crescent Societies will need to carefully match their resources to both the needs of others and to opportunities. They will have to find and nurture effective partners in the poorer countries with which they plan to work. They will have to train and educate staff and field workers in these new ways of viewing disasters.

Perhaps most important, they will have to spend time and money educating the general public, the source of both the funds and the human concern which drives the relief agencies. This public — in both the industrialised and the developing countries — must come to see disasters not simply as "acts of God" striking helpless people, but as the results of the complex ways in which people operate within their environment. They must come to understand that charity and concern are most effective when they begin before, not after, the disaster.

But it is not only the relief agencies who must critically analyse their policies and practices. The rapid increase in disasters in many Third World countries makes it necessary to question current development practices, for some of these disaster trends bear evidence of development programmes that have gone wrong. Governments as well as development authorities — within the UN system and outside — will want to take note of these trends and work together to combat them.

As has been shown, most disaster victims are to be found among the poorest of the poor. Governments as well as most Northern donors usually claim that their main target groups are the rural poor. If this is true, much more emphasis ought to be given to disaster prevention, as such programmes can be an effective way to assist the poor. Over the last decades, the great majority of development assistance has been allocated for industrial and urban projects. Far too little attention has been given to the problems of the many rural poor. On average only about 10-15% of the total investments in most poor countries have been directed towards rural projects.

Today more and more experts question past policies. Food production does not keep pace with population growth, particularly in Africa, making many poor countries heavily dependent on food imports even during "normal" harvest years. When disasters strike, the situation becomes unmanageable.

Rural development — which includes protection and rehabilitation of land, soil, water and forests — offers part of the solution to these problems.

"The biosphere seldom presents human society with imperatives; rather we face choices about the sort of world we want to live in", wrote US environmentalist Erik Eckholm in *Down to Earth* (Pluto Press; Norton,

1982). "Responses to environmental threats can be formulated only in relation to broader human goals. The issue is not whether societies can adapt to further environmental degradation, but what the price of doing so will be.... In the struggle to create a more decent, a more human world, the environmental factor is gradually receiving its due respect."

 **Appendix**

On 12-14 June 1984, the Swedish Red Cross invited leaders of international and national relief, development and environmental organisations to Lidingö, Sweden, for a two-day meeting to discuss its report, *Prevention Better than Cure,* the main findings of which are reflected in this book. The participants came from government and United Nations bodies, from non-governmental organisations and from the Red Cross movement. Statements by participants (extracts from some of them are given below) show that organisations viewing disasters from many different perspectives have arrived by different paths at the same basic conclusions:

* Human beings are playing a growing role in causing 'natural disasters', largely by ways in which they alter their environment.
* While relief remains important, it cannot by itself begin to cope with the disaster processes at work in the Third World.
* Long-term efforts are required.
* For these to be successful, the many organisations concerned with developing nations must work together.

—oooOOOooo—

Mr Lennart Bodström, Swedish Minister for Foreign Affairs:
"The emergency situation in many parts of the world at present — particularly in Africa — calls for comprehensive, well-coordinated programmes, if durable solutions are to be found. The whole spectrum of problems cannot be solved by one agency or by one type of resources. The necessary development process must be the concerted work of voluntary agencies, UN organisations, international financing bodies, the donor and the recipient governments and, last but not least, of the people themselves.

The Red Cross study on emergency assistance very rightly gives high priority to ecological aspects. There is no doubt that the spread of deserts, the plunder of forests, salination and other signs of degradation of soils are some of our earth's major problems."

Mr M'Hamed Essaafi, disaster relief co-ordinator, UN Disaster Relief Organisation:

"In our relief work we are fighting a losing battle. Disaster relief must be continued and developed. But some new aspects — preparedness and prevention — must be added."

Mr Manfred A. Max-Neef, managing director, CEPAUR, Santiago, Chile:

"The developed countries force the Third World to pay back their debts. The only way they can do that is producing cash crops. Cash-cropping prevents subsistence farming. The alternative to paying unpayable debts is committing suicide. What is most important, our banking system or the human beings?...

"Governments want to build dams and other prestige projects, or to be superpowers. There is often no point in discussing ecology with them."

Mr Guy Stringer, Director, OXFAM:

"Badly planned development work has caused much damage... We must aim at the rural poor. They are brave, they work hard. And behind them an increasing number of urban poor are waiting for our assistance."

Mr Brian Walker, director, Independent Commission on International Humanitarian Issues:

"Now the whole system will begin to move. There is so far no forum where all aspects are brought together — aid, development, environment. The most important thing is to bring these things together...

"Capacity and willingness to cooperate — that is the critical point. It is missing in all our work."

Mme Sall (née Tokosselle Sy), President, Mauritanian Red Crescent Society:

"Drought is slow and silent and does not draw the attention of the international public. Three years ago it was not yet a disaster in my country. I tried to alert the opinion so that we could prevent one. But no one would listen. People have to die first. But we have to start at an earlier stage."

Mr K.P. Wagner, Chief, Office for Special Relief Operations, UN Food and Agriculture Organization:

"A joint approach is necessary. It can't go on like this any further."

Mr Anders Forsse, Director General, Swedish International Development
Authority:
  "SIDA is eager to support this new opening, and also needs support
  from the NGOs in the recruiting of personnel...
  "Host governments' attitudes are important. They are often
  unwilling or incapable. And if so nobody, not even the Red Cross, can
  get anywhere...
  "...don't always find it easy to stick to long-rate programmes."

Mr James C. Ingram, Executive Director, UN World Food Programme:
  "A strategy for disaster-vulnerable countries is required."

Mr Hans Christian Bugge, Secretary General, Redd Barna (Save the
Children), Norway:
  "What methods can we develop not to undermine the built-in forces
  in a group of people when we give short-term relief assistance? I don't
  think we have the methods yet."

Mr Unto Korhonen, Ambassador, FINNIDA (the Finnish aid agency):
  "Coordination of aid is very important. At least we have to know what
  other agencies are doing and how."

Mrs Kerstin Oldfelt, Director, Regional Office for Europe, UN Environment
Programme:
  "It is very difficult to influence governments. Poor people don't have
  strong voices. And people that are aware on a country-level don't have
  any influence either. Structures must be built to bring about influence.
  The Red Cross has a strong network."

Mr Gösta Edgren, Under-Secretary of State for International Development
Cooperation, Swedish Ministry for Foreign Affairs:
  "We are moving towards a new concept of the relationship between
  emergency relief and development aid, a concept which recognises that
  some of the occurrences which we have referred to as disasters or
  emergencies are really semi-permanent phenomena which must be
  attacked with measures of both types, in a more deliberate manner...
  "If we can assume that disasters of the type we have witnessed over
  the past decades are a recurrent rather than an abnormal phenomenon,
  it is impossible at length to separate disaster relief from development
  management in general, administratively or in terms of programming
  and budgeting...
  "Medium and long-term development projects must be more closely

directed towards removing the root causes of the recurrent or 'creeping' emergencies, be they floods, drought or civil unrest....

"Gradually, the emphasis in the bilateral aid programme has shifted from new investment for instance in industry and social services to utilisation and maintenance of existing facilities. Conservation and regeneration of natural resources has been given increasing weight in rural development. These trends will have to be strengthened in future, even if it has to be done at the expense of more capital-intensive lines of activity in manufacturing and infrastructure. The overriding strategic objective of Swedish aid to disaster-prone countries should be to assist them in restructuring their economies so as to become less vulnerable to different forms of 'creeping emergencies'...."

Mr James A. Lee, Environmental Adviser, World Bank:

"We must recognise and treat the critical points in the chain of events that lead to disasters. Metaphorically, we must shift our energies from rescuing flood victims to planting trees... Expertise and money from institutions in the industrialised nations for economic development projects that are sensitive to local ecological, social and economic requirements can bring improvements and benefits that can be sustained far beyond the lifetimes of recent, massive projects of the kind cited where these requirements were not heeded...

"Unless and until economic development, whatever its auspice and source of financing, recognises the 'disaster-prone' consequences of failing to identify and provide for the untoward environmental consequences that often accompany it, your (the Red Cross) job will become ever harder, more costly and less able to meet the human suffering that disasters bring...

"No one is so naive to propose that changing the course of history will be easy. The forces behind population growth, unsound resource use and development, and the disasters they can cause are enormously powerful. But I believe that we can avert these disasters only by dedicating our resources and talents to get at the root causes."

—oooOOOooo—

The two-day meeting ended with a statement by all of the participants.

1.   The symposium supports the Report by the Swedish Red Cross, *Prevention Better than Cure.*

2. We urge the Swedish Red Cross to advocate the message of the Report throughout the League of Red Cross and Red Crescent Societies, with a view to securing policy decisions by the League in favour of linking disaster relief to developmental and environmental strategies and, furthermore, in stimulating public opinion, in both donor and recipient countries, in these matters.

3. We further urge the Red Cross and Red Crescent Societies to cooperate with other developmental and environmental agencies in pursuit of these objectives.

In addition to the formal statement, participants agreed on the following points:

1. Prevention projects are indispensable. Development programmes in general should focus more on root causes of disasters; small-scale projects at the village level are preferable; it is necessary to start broad prevention programmes with strong inter-agency cooperation in certain regions where the situation is difficult.

2. Information/awareness programmes should be intensified in order to establish awareness of the environmental issues within host governments and among the public at large, in both industrial and Third World countries.

3. Relief operations should be improved:

   * Relief efforts should be regarded as an opportunity to start development work.
   * Considerations should be given to environmental factors in all relief planning.
   * Preparedness programmes should include environmental considerations.
   * Relief funds should be used more flexibly, i.e. for development purposes and in particular for prevention measures.

4. Special training/education programmes on prevention should be developed for industrial countries as well as for Third World countries.

5. Non-governmental organisations are very important for the further implementation of the outlined measures.

—oooOOOooo—

144

Participants at the symposium were:

Food and Agriculture Organization	Mr K.P. Wagner Chief, Office for Special Relief Operations	Ethiopian Red Cross Society
		Indian Red Cross Society
Independent Commission on International Humanitarian Issues	Mr Brian Walker Director	
United Nations Disaster Relief Organisation	Mr M'Hamed Essaafi Under-Secretary General Disaster Relief Co-ordinator	Mauritanian Red Crescent Society
		Swiss Red Cross Society
United Nations Environment Programme	Mrs Kerstin Oldfelt Director, Regional Office for Europe	Zimbabwe Red Cross Society
UNICEF	Mr Bertil Mathsson Secretary of the Executive Board	Uganda Red Cross Society
	Mr Hank Davelaar	Swedish Red Cross Society
World Food Programme	Mr James C. Ingram Executive Director	
	Mr Mohamed Zejjari Senior Project Management Officer	
World Bank	Dr James Lee Environmental Adviser	
International Committee of the Red Cross	Mr Philippe Dind Deputy Director, Operations Department	
International Union for the Conservation of Nature and Natural Resources	Mr M.J. Cockerell Director	
League of Red Cross and Red Crescent Societies	Mr Hans Høegh Secretary General	Canadian International Development Agency
	Mr Richard Bergstrom Under-Secretary General	
	Mr Stephen Davey Head of Eastern and Southern Africa Department	DANINDA
OXFAM	Mr Guy Stringer Director	FINNIDA
World Wildlife Fund	Mr Frank Schmidt Assistant Director General	NORAD
Danish Red Cross Society	Nr Eigil Pedersen Secretary General	Swedish International Development Agency
Finnish Red Cross Society	Mr Kai Warras Secretary General	
Icelandic Red Cross Society	Mr Jon Asgeirsson Secretary General	
Norwegian Red Cross Society	Mr Odd Grann Secretary General	Relief and Rehabilitation Commission

Mr Dawit Zawde
Chairman

Shri Ajit Bhowmick
Secretary General

Shri G.C. Baveja
Honorary Treasurer

Madame Sall, née Tokosselle Sy
President

Mr Anton Wenger
Relief Co-ordinator

Mr Olivier Kuwana
Secretary General

Mr Erisa Kironde
Chairman

Mr Börje Wallberg
Chairman

Mrs Gudrun Göransson
First Vice Chairman

Mr Anders Wijkman
Secretary General

Mr Claes-Göran Landergren
League Chief Delegate, Ethiopia

Mr Christian Kornevall
Acting Head, International Department

Mr Gunnar Hagman
Project Leader
Swedcross Disaster Survey

Mr William McWhinney
Senior Vice-President

Mr Jean Devlin
Coordinator of International Humanitarian Assistance

Ms Suzanne Rubow
Member of the Board

Mr Unto Korhonen
Ambassador

Mr Niels L. Dahl
Ambassador

Mr Anders Forsse
Director General

Mr Kurt Kristiansson
Head of Disaster Relief Section

Mr Johan Holmberg
Head of Agriculture Division

Mr Taye Gurmu
Deputy Commissioner

Ministry for Foreign Affairs

Swedish Parliament

Swedish University of
Agricultural Sciences

The Royal Swedish Academy
of Sciences

Centre for Science and
Environment, New Delhi

League of Red Cross
Societies

Växjö, Sweden

Redd Barna
Oslo, Norway

The Beijer Institute
Stockholm

Senior Adviser to the Food
and Agriculture Organization
Athens

Centre for Study & Promotion
of Urban, Rural & Development
Alternatives
Santiago, Chile

The Swedish Society for the
Conservation of Nature

Project Adviser to the
Swedish Red Cross

World Commission on
Environment and Development

Mr Tom Tscherning
Deputy Under-Secretary of State

Mrs Marika Fahlén
Head of Section

Mrs Karin Söder
Mrs Margaretha af Ugglas
Mr Jan Erik Wikström
Mr Olle Göransson
Mr Sture Korpås

Prof. Mårten Carlsson
Rector

Mr Sven Pellbäck
Head of International Rural
Development Center

Prof. Per Wramner
Institute for Ecology and
Environmental Care

Prof. Tord Ganelius
Secretary General

Mr Anil Agarwal
Director

Mr Henrik Beer
Secretary General Emeritus

Prof. Mårten Bendz

Mr Hans Christian Bugge
Secretary General

Mr Gordon Goodman
Director

Dr Sture Linnér

Mr Manfred A. Max-Neef
Managing Director

Mr Mats Segnestam
Executive Director

Mr Jürgen Weyand

Mr Bertil Hägerhäll
Director

Further reading

CENTRE FOR SCIENCE AND ENVIRONMENT. *The State of India's Environment: 1982*. Centre for Science and Environment (1982).

CUNY, Frederick C. *Disasters and Development*. Oxford University Press, Oxford (1983).

DAVIS, Ian. *Shelter after Disaster*. Oxford Polytechnic Press, Oxford (1980).

ECKHOLM, Erik. *Down to Earth*. Pluto Press, London; W.W. Norton, New York (1982).

FRANCIS, Peter. *Volcanoes*. Penguin Books Ltd, Harmondsworth, Middlesex, (1976).

GRAINGER, Alan. *Desertification: how people make deserts, how people can stop and why they don't*. Earthscan, London (1982).

HAGMAN, Gunnar. *Prevention Better than Cure*. Swedish Red Cross, Stockholm (1984).

HEWITT, K. (Ed). *Interpretations of Calamity*. Allen & Unwin, Boston (1983).

PRYOR, L.D. *Ecological Mismanagement in Natural Disasters*. International Union for Conservation of Nature and Natural Resources, Commission of Ecology Papers No 2, Gland, Switzerland (1982).

SEN, Amartya. *Poverty and Famines: An Essay on Entitlement and Deprivation*. Clarendon Press, Oxford (1981).

TWOSE, Nigel. *Behind the Weather; why the Poor Suffer Most: Drought and the Sahel*. OXFAM, Oxford (1984).

VERNEY, Peter. *The Earthquake Handbook*. Paddington, London (1979).

WALTHAM, Tony. *Catastrophe: the violent earth*. Macmillan, London (1978).

WARD, Roy. *Flood: a geographical perspective*. Macmillan, London (1978).

WHITTOW, John. *Disasters: the Anatomy of Environmental Hazards*. Penguin Books Ltd, Harmondsworth, Middlesex (1980).

EARTHSCAN PAPERBACKS

A Village in a Million by Sumi Chauhan   1979   £2.00/$5.00

Climate and Mankind by John Gribbin   1979   £2.00/$5.00

Antarctica and its Resources by Barbara Mitchell and Jon Tinker
1980   £2.50/$6.25

*Mud, mud — The potential of earth-based materials for Third World
housing* by Anil Agarwal   1981   £2.50/$6.25   Also in French &
Spanish

New and Renewable Energies 1 (solar, biomass) edited by Jon Tinker
1981   £2.50/$6.25   Also in French & Spanish

New and Renewable Energies 2 (others) edited by Jon Tinker   1981
£2.50/$6.25   Also in French & Spanish

*Water, Sanitation, Health — for All? Prospects for the International
Drinking Water Supply and Sanitation Decade, 1981-90* by Anil
Agarwal, James Kimondo, Gloria Moreno and Jon Tinker.   1981
£3.00/$7.00

Carbon Dioxide, Climate and Man by John Gribbin   1981
£2.50/$6.25

Fuel Alcohol: Energy and Environment in a Hungry World by Bill
Kovarik   1982   £3.00/$7.00

*Stockholm Plus Ten: Promises, Promises? The decade since the 1972
UN Environment Conference* by Robin Clarke and Lloyd Timberlake
1982   £3.00/$7.00

Tropical Moist Forests: The Resource, The People, The Threat by
Catherine Caufield   1982   £3.00/$7.00   Also in French & Spanish

What's Wildlife Worth? by Robert and Christine Prescott-Allen   1982
£3.00/$7.00   Also in Spanish

*Desertification — how people make deserts, how people can stop and
why they don't* by Alan Grainger   1982   £3.00/$7.00   Also in
French

Gasifiers: fuel for siege economies by Gerald Foley, Geoffrey Barnard and Lloyd Timberlake   1983   £3.00/$7.00

Genes from the wild — using wild genetic resources for food and raw materials by Robert and Christine Prescott-Allen   1983   £3.00/$7.00

A million villages, a million Decades? The World Water and Sanitation Decade from two South Indian villages — Guruvarajapalayam and Vellakal by Sumi Krishna Chauhan and K. Gopalakrishnan   1983   £3.00/$7.00

Who puts the water in the taps? Community participation in Third World drinking water, sanitation and health by Sumi Krishna Chauhan with Zhang Bihua, K. Gopalakrishnan, Lala Rukh Hussain, Ajoa Yeboah-Afari and Francisco Leal   1984   £3.00/$7.00

Stoves and trees by Gerald Foley, Patricia Moss and Lloyd Timberlake 1984   £3.50/$7.00

Fuelwood: the energy crisis that won't go away by Erik Eckholm, Gerald Foley, Geoffrey Barnard and Lloyd Timberlake   1984   £3.50/$7.00

Natural disasters: Acts of God or acts of Man? by Anders Wijkman and Lloyd Timberlake   1984   Also in Spanish £3.50/$7.00

Urban land and shelter for the poor by Patrick McAuslan   1985   £3.50/$7.00

All Earthscan publications are available from:

Earthscan
3 Endsleigh Street
London WC1H ODD, UK

Earthscan Washington Bureau
1717 Massachusetts Avenue NW
Washington DC 20036, USA